ECOLOGICAL INTELLIGENCE
REDISCOVERING OURSELVES IN NATURE

IAN M^CCALLUM

WITH A FOREWORD BY LYALL WATSON

AFRICA
Geographic

Africa Geographic
P O Box 44223, Claremont 7735, Cape Town, South Africa
www.africageographic.com

Registration number 92/05883/07

First published in 2005
Reprinted in 2005, 2006

Copyright © Ian McCallum

Editor: Di Paice
Production editor: Mary Duncan
Permissions: Shelley Prince
Design, layout & production: Gillian Black & Alessandro Bonora
Cover photograph: Ian McCallum
Back cover portrait: Sharon McCallum
Cover reproduction by Resolution Colour (Pty) Ltd
Printed by Paarl Print (Pty) Ltd

Also by Ian McCallum (www.inventafrica.com)
Wild Gifts and *Thorns to Kilimanjaro*

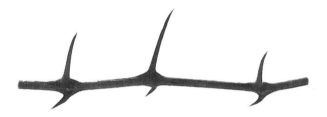

The thorns of the tree, **Ziziphus mucronata**, are spaced along the length of every branch in pairs. One of the pair points robustly outward and forward while the other curves back and inwards in the opposite direction. The Nguni African legend says the thorns tell us something about ourselves – that we must look ahead to the future ... but we must never forget where we have come from.

CONTENTS

ACKNOWLEDGEMENTS

THIS BOOK WOULD NOT HAVE BEEN POSSIBLE WITHOUT THE ADVICE, support and inspiration of the following remarkable people: Peter Borchert, Alessandro Bonora, Gillian Black, Mary Duncan and Shelley Prince of Africa Geographic, Anne Anderson, Jean Badenhorst, Chris Bakkes, Joan Berning, Antony Burgmans, George Ellis, Barbara Fairhead, Chic and Danna Flack, Brian Gaze, Michelle and Steve Henley, Map Ives, Lochie Jacobs, Dereck and Beverley Joubert, Festus Mbinga, Marlene McCay, Ian McMillan and Ian Michler of Invent Africa, Gus Mills, Jock and Rosie Orford, Di Paice, Nita Permuy, Peter and Beverly Pickford, Ian Player and the Wilderness Foundation, Felicity Swanson, Hermann Wessels, Lyall Watson and Grant Woodrow.

A special thank you to my editor, Di Paice, and to Felicity Swanson, who was an essential part of the flow and early formatting of this book.

To the wild animals of the Okavango and of the Linyanti in northern Botswana, thank you for sharing your river with me and for helping me to redefine the word "intelligence".

To Colin Bell, Malcolm McCullough and Grant Woodrow of Wilderness Safaris, thank you for making my Linyanti adventures possible.

To the many Botswana guides with whom I have worked – Greg Hughes, Vundi Kashamba, Marks Kehaletse, Bolatotswe Makgetho, Copper Malela, Frank Mashebe, Mike Myers, Moses Ntema, Clinton Phillips, James Pisetu, Isaac Seredile and Maipaa Tekanyetso – thank you for what we have shared.

Finally, to my best friend and wife, Sharon – thank you for your love, your generosity of spirit, your patience, your attention to detail and the countless hours you spent reading and re-reading the manuscripts that gave rise to this book.

ecology [ee kol o ji] *n* – study of the relations of living organisms to their
environment; study of ecosystems; study of the environmental conditions of existence
(Croal and Rankin)

intelligence [in telli jans] *n* – the capacity to learn from experience, to think
in abstract or symbolic terms and to deal effectively with one's environment
(Atkinson, Smith, Hilgard). The capacity of an animal to use tools, to solve problems,
to find its way home and to learn by imitation
(Hauser)

This book is dedicated to three strange angels –
the naturalist, the scientist and the poet in all of us

WILDERNESS

Have we forgotten
that wilderness is not a place,
but a pattern of soul
where every tree, every bird and beast
is a soul maker?

Have we forgotten
that wilderness is not a place
but a moving feast of stars,
footprints, scales and beginnings?

Since when
did we become afraid of the night
and that only the bright stars count?
Or that our moon is not a moon
unless it is full?

By whose command
were the animals
through groping fingers,
one for each hand,
reduced to the big and little five?

Have we forgotten
that every creature is within us
carried by tides
of Earthly blood
and that we named them?

Have we forgotten
that wilderness is not a place,
but a season
and that we are in its
final hour?

FOREWORD

We are connected with each other in surprising ways.

I LEARNT THIS WHEN I WAS JUST EIGHT YEARS OLD, A CURIOUS CHILD taking pleasure in wandering barefoot and alone across the great Karoo, semi-desert plain that covers most of South Africa's dry interior.

At first acquaintance these are bleak places, rusty and unforgiving, stretching to horizons broken only by occasional flat-topped stone koppies. But like all deserts, their delights lie in the detail.

Every day I discovered something new. Floral stones sculpted by the sun and wind and, between them, a wonderful variety of succulent plants camouflaged to look like pebbles waiting patiently for the next rare fall of rain. And once in a while I would be encouraged to encounter a whip-tailed lizard, a trap-door spider, or even a fossil shell left behind by an ancient sea.

These signs of life delighted me. They promised continuity, but I was totally unprepared for what I stumbled over one cloudless day...

It was a shiny stone, larger than my foot, one amongst many others, polished by the elements with reflective 'desert varnish'. But this one was different. It was golden and beautifully shaped with the sort of symmetry that set it apart from the others. More than just a stone.

I knelt to get a closer look and for a long time that was all I dared to do. I was afraid to touch it, but eventually my curiosity overcame my hesitance and I put my hand gently on it. And as I did, every hair on the nape of my neck bristled.

I knew what it was! A hand-axe, carefully crafted to fit even my small hand. A message from the Stone Age, passed directly from the maker's hand to mine across the gap of a million years.

I learnt much later that tools of this kind were manufactured by *Homo erectus* who used it as an all-purpose instrument for throwing, hammering, skinning, cutting and scraping. The Palaeolithic equivalent of a Swiss Army knife. Something made and used on the spot, or carried to the next site if it was found to be especially pleasing.

I still have this strange gift on my desk and it now fits my hand like a glove, continuing to give me great pleasure. To me it proves that intelligence is not peculiar to our species. It is the product of collecting, collating, crafting a deliberate choice, a work of art and early science.

This is what Ian McCallum calls Ecological Intelligence – involving 'Rediscovering Ourselves in Nature'. And it seems to me that his insights are the product of three skills.

Ian is a physician who doesn't believe that there are any quick medical fixes, nor any easy ways to heal, for ourselves or our environments. But like Pythagorus, he suggests that everything is intelligent in its own way. He practices remedies that involve our return to nature. He encourages the rediscovery of our place in the world, and he teaches the restoration of 'soul places' whose absence from our lives are a direct cause of homesickness.

He is also a Jungian practitioner. He understands the importance and significance of having both a Collective Unconscious and a personal Shadow. Armed thus he has a sound and balanced sense of Evolutionary History, vital to understanding some of the mysteries inherent in the construction of weaverbird nests, termite mounds, shoaling fish and all the other 'ideas' that help a number of species to compete in their Darwinian struggles for survival.

But perhaps most important of all, Ian is a published poet, a romantic who is not afraid to stretch scientific horizons and is uniquely qualified to deal with the paradoxes that run wild in the mindfield that lies between the extremes which science is forced to confront in questions involving the existence of mind.

I admire this brave attempt to tackle a very difficult subject which sheds new light on James Lovelock's forecast that through human beings, the Earth may have its best chance of becoming conscious of itself.

LYALL WATSON
Ireland, 2005

I am the keeper of the zoo: I say yes and no:
I sing and kill and work...
Carl Sandburg

We are a poetic species
Richard Rorty

INTRODUCTION

TOWARD A GREATER AWARENESS OF THE PRIVILEGE OF WHAT IT MEANS TO be the human animal is what this book is about. To me, it is a wild and ethical imperative – an urgent reminder that we are inextricably linked to the land; that the history of every living creature is within us; that we are above all a mindful, poetic species and that we are the "keepers of our zoo". If we cannot accept this then we will continue to be the creatures of our own undoing.

When we review the history of life on this planet, it is evident that death and, eventually, extinction is the fate of all species and that life, with a will of its own, will continue to find new ways of expressing itself. This in itself is a miracle. But there is another side to this awesome process. Prior to the emergence of humans, nowhere in the evolutionary narrative does it show any one species contributing quite so dramatically to its own extinction, let alone to the extinction of other species such as birds, butterflies and marine animals, plants and beetles, as well as many species we don't even know about.

There is hardly a place on the face of our planet that we have not explored, settled and altered in some way to satisfy our own ends, and the news is not good. The denuding of tropical forests, acid rain, air and water pollution, and diminishing wilderness areas, the introduction of alien vegetation and green house warming all have one thing in common – the human factor. A sobering thought. Even more sobering is the realisation that the natural selection process of evolution is happening right in front of our eyes and we are the force behind it. In response to the well-intentioned use of insecticides, antibiotics and other organic chemicals, the Earth is now host to multiple new strains of "resistant" organisms, from bacteria and viruses to weeds and insects, including more than a hundred new strains of DDT-resistant mosquitoes. Having turned a blind eye to the fact that we are a part of Nature's great diversity, we have become ecologically unintelligent. Lopsided in favour of the angels, we have steadily distanced ourselves from our biological past. In what is sometimes referred to as the Human-Nature split, we have ignorantly, if not arrogantly, placed ourselves at the apex of creation. It is time to come down from that precarious pedestal.

The big question, of course, is: can we reverse this destructive, self-deceptive trend? Are we willing to come off that pedestal? Something in me says no. It is difficult to counter the argument that the downward spiral of human co-existence with this planet has already begun and that it is too late to make amends; but something in me says yes. It is that something that allows me to continue my work as a psychiatrist, that affirms the belief that when we commit ourselves, we can learn to see ourselves differently. That it is in our nature to change, to adapt, to diversify, to deal with suffering and to discover, with time, that our suffering is sometimes an important part of our healing. It is a belief that the future of human co-existence with the Earth is going to depend just as much on the creativity of its scientists and poets as it does on changes in climate and vegetation. And so, if it is not too late, how do we begin to rediscover ourselves in Nature? How do we begin to heal or to reconcile the Human-Nature split?

First of all, we have to stop speaking about the Earth being in need of healing. The Earth doesn't need healing. We do. Utterly indifferent to human existence, the Earth will thrive – when we are gone. We are the ones who need to redefine our relationship with it. We are the ones who have become ashamed of our wild nature, and by this I do not mean the coarse, aggressive and self-destructive sense of the word. That is savagery. Instead, we have become apologetic for being dispassionate, spontaneous, raw, territorial, protective and angry. We are the ones who need to do the reaching out, not to save the Earth, but to rediscover ourselves in it.

Healing and mending are often regarded as being the same thing but it is going to be important that we understand the distinction between the two. Healing seldom occurs, if at all, without a profound change in attitude not only to oneself and to the world, but to oneself in the world. Mending – the quick fix – on the other hand, is something else. As necessary and as convenient as it may be, it seldom makes any demand on one's capacity to reflect or to change one's ways.

Secondly, if we are serious about the healing of the Human-Nature split it is essential that we become more evolutionary minded. We have to wake up to the privilege of what it means to be human: that we are part of a web of life in which everything is genetically and molecularly linked and that human psychology has deep evolutionary roots. We are naturally resistant to change, let alone to admitting our animal past. And yet the evidence is there. With the unravelling of the human genome and the subsequent discovery that more than ninety percent of it is shared with every other mammal, the poets and the old shamans have been proven right. The animals are our soul mates and we are the human animal.

And then there is our link to the Earth itself. I believe that our identity is intimately associated with a deep historical sense of continuity with wild places and the animals that live there – that we have an ancient, genetic memory of where we have come from. These are the places that permit us to say, sometimes unreservedly, "it is as if this place is in my blood ... it is as if I have come home".

To lose one's sense of union with wild places is to pre-empt what I believe is one of the most overlooked conditions in modern psychiatry – homesickness. Often presenting as a restless depression, homesickness and a loss of wildness are the same thing. So is a loss of soul. Our creativity suffers and so do our relationships. Anyone who vaguely understands the significance of "walk-about" or who longs for the chilling night call of the spotted hyena, *Crocus crocuta*, or the shape and the shade of the Umbrella Thorn tree, *Acacia tortilis*, will know that restlessness. It is also likely that they will understand the unmistakable homesickness in these lines by the poet, Rainer Maria Rilke:

> Sometimes a man stands up during supper,
> and walks outdoors and keeps on walking,
> because of a church that stands somewhere in the East.

The cure for homesickness is to remember where we have come from. It is to rediscover that original church within oneself and to remember that the wild areas of the world are the landscapes of the soul and that the creatures who belong there are soul-makers. We need these places in much the same way that the ancient Celts needed their sacred groves – not because they are there, or because they are beautiful, but for that compulsive union of fact and feeling that we experience when we go there. Deeply visceral, it is the experience of soul. And it is impossible to put a price on it. To remember that church is not enough. We have to be able to go there, also. Be it the desert, the savannah, the mountains, the sea or the wild lands of ice and snow, we have to be able to go to the places where we most belong and where we are most ourselves. It is an inner and an outer journey and our healing depends on both.

To be aware of the evolutionary roots of human psychology is to deepen one's understanding of what is loosely referred to as human nature. Without this understanding, an ecological intelligence is impossible. Unwilling to look at ourselves, we have become masters in the art of finger pointing and self-deception and until we understand the origins and the dynamics of why we do it, any attempt to reconcile the Human-Nature split is going to be futile. It is essential, therefore, that we develop a greater awareness of the structure and functioning of the human psyche, particularly the workings of the human ego – what we refer to as "me", what it is, how it has evolved, how it defends itself, how blind it can be and yet how essential it is for our survival. Yes, the human animal is a deeply biological being, but we are psychological beings also, creatures that reflect, fantasize, hope, intuit, pray, bless, blame, care, cheat, love and who look for the meanings in things.

To me, psychology begins to make more sense when seen through an evolutionary eye. It comes into its own when we become aware of the universality of the various strategies of survival – the way all animals consciously and unconsciously encounter the world. Say what you wish, we are survivors – the living evidence of more than two million years of hominin existence and with it a consciousness that has become not only self-aware, but aware of the awareness of others.

Derived from the Greek word *psyche*, which means soul, breath or life, human psychology is the science that studies the conscious and unconscious workings of the human psyche, especially our behavioural and mental processes. It includes the study of thoughts, emotions, feelings, memory, personality and relationships – not only the way we relate to people, places and events, but to the way we relate to ourselves. It is the study of human nature. It is not an exact science and probably never will be, which is why for many scientists it is regarded as being too abstract or too theoretical to be relevant to empirical science. It is essential that this attitude be changed, for not only are we all naturalists of sorts, all of us scientifically curious, we are also philosophers and psychologists, if only in a small way. And what is more, we can't help it! It is in our nature to be objective, to explore, to measure and to define our outer world, but this is only a part of our nature. Human nature is powerfully subjective too; it is both abstract and abstracting, never entirely satisfied with what can be measured, which is why, for everything wonderful about science, somehow it seldom answers the deep, existential questions in our lives.

How, for example, can one possibly discredit those great poetic dimensions of human society – spirit and soul? We readily speak of the spirit of adventure and the spirit of science, of soul mates, soul places and the dark night of the soul. The words are at the tips of our tongues. They are intrinsic to our descriptions of kinship, belonging, connection and continuity. And we know what they mean, even if we cannot fully explain them. They may well be linked to neuro-circuits, neurotransmitters and circulating hormones, as I am sure they are, but *how* they are linked and to which combinations of circuits or neurochemicals, we'll probably never know. It would seem they can't be measured, or better still, they refuse to be measured. Does that make them any less real or, indeed, irrelevant? I think not. Instead, because they are dimensions that are experienced and which add to our sense of meaning, they need to be understood as psychologically significant and therefore valid.

And then there is language. If we are serious about rediscovering ourselves in Nature, we are going to need a language that speaks for science and soul, that narrows the gap between subject and object, that slips between yes and no. We will need a language that continually reminds us of where we have come from and of what we have to do if we are to become ecologically intelligent. For the time being, the only language I know that can begin to do this is poetry. It may be an extravagant claim, but there is a history to it ...

At the end of 1997, after eight years of working with troubled adolescents and mentally handicapped children, I resigned from my post as the head of the Child, Family and Adolescent Unit at the Lentegeur Psychiatric Hospital in Cape Town. My wife and I headed off to the Linyanti wilderness of northern Botswana where, working as a guide and co-manager of a small tented lodge, I was overwhelmed by a sense that I had "come home". I tried to keep a diary, but every time I tried to write down my experiences with animals, it came out in stanza-form. Prose somehow escaped me. Instead, what I was writing was verse – "pure nonsense ... pure wisdom" as the Chilean poet Pablo Neruda said of his first written lines. Where did it come from? I don't know. Gripped by them, it was as if the poems were writing me. I tried to ignore them, but it didn't work. Some of them came quickly, decisively. Some of them refused to be rushed, waiting instead until I was ready for them. Others wrestled with me, sometimes deep into the night. I came to see them as wild gifts.

> To begin
> to know wilderness,
> something in me had to die –
> the pregnant parts,
> the motherly expectations
> and the test tube notions
> of a safe delivery.

In the wild
dead foetuses are for real,
vultures are the midwives of new life
And to be abandoned is to grow.

To begin
to know wilderness,
something in me had to come alive –
my wild side,
the part that knows
that it is impossible to sleep with the dead
without being awakened by them.

In the wild
the animal spirits are for real
they are the shadows in our bones
and they come to us
as wild gifts.

To rediscover ourselves in Nature does not mean turning one's back on technology as is often advocated. Technology is part of our nature. It is part of the evolution of a problem-solving, tool-making species. The harnessing of the molecular formulae of genes, medicinal plants, hormones and tissue extracts to enhance the quality of life of countless human and non-human beings has to be understood as being just as significant as the harnessing of fire by our ancestors *Homo erectus* less than a million years ago. Without technology we could not speak about DNA, there would be no photographs of Earth from space, no understanding of the AIDS virus and no long distance calls from a daughter on her travels in a foreign land. Without technology the monitoring and protection of many of the world's endangered species would be impossible. Celebrate it. Learn how to say yes and no to it.

Throughout this book I have used the paired words 'yes' and 'no' for two very specific reasons. The first is to encourage the reader to become a little more comfortable with paradox – discovering the sometimes irrational yet meaningful truths that are hidden in statements that are seemingly contradictory or absurd. Science has long been familiar with paradox, for example Chaos Theory and with it the recognition that there are patterns of order in what we all too readily interpret as chaotic. And then there is the paradox of the dual perception of light – that it can be perceived as being either waves or particles. The paired words, then, are not mutually exclusive. Instead, they convey a simple wisdom: everything is in process ... every idea, every interpretation and every strategy has at least two sides. The second reason is to remind the reader that yes and no are the two most powerful words in the vocabulary of a species that has become capable of deciding what to do about its future.

PART ONE

REMEMBERING WHERE
WE HAVE COME FROM

Hinged to far beginnings
pulled by a distant sun
we are linked to the scars
on the moon.

Astonishing! Everything is intelligent!

Pythagoras

1

THE RESHAPING OF MYTH AND LANGUAGE

THERE IS NOT A CULTURE IN THE WORLD THAT DOES NOT HAVE MYTHS, legends or fairytales – explanations, no matter how fantastic, of the origins of the world and of life, of heroes and villains, of how we ought to behave and how not to. While many of them are based on elements of fact, they nevertheless acquire a peculiar potency. Embellished by the human imagination, they often represent a highly invested truth for a group or an individual. This means that they must never be negated as being mere figments of the imagination.

Any story that begins "Once upon a time ..." is magnetically charged with this potency. It draws us into the narrative that follows and the reason for this is that we inevitably discover within them our own life narratives. The hero and the heroine is in all of us. So is the victim, and believe it or not, the villain too. Myths and legends are the carriers of meaning and the quest for meaning is one of the most defining characteristics of the human animal. Myths have a profound psychological significance. We are shaped and guided by them. However, we sculpt them also. We give them new clothes and new voices. We not only derive meaning from myths, but we add meaning to them, too. As hard as we try to dismiss them, they refuse to go away. "They are insidious" says the Canadian psychiatrist, Vivian Rakoff, "great secret dragons which may appear to be slain and discredited, but which mysteriously reappear as powerful as ever to press their perennial claim to a territory of belief and understanding."

Nearly all of our scientific theories have a subjective core and they almost all originate from intuition and myth, said the great twentieth century philosopher of science Karl Popper. For example, the "bushman" hunter-gatherers of the Kalahari knew nothing of the shared genes between humans and animals, but their thirty-thousand-year mythology tells us that all living things are connected. They have been proven right. And what about Empedocles, whose intuition thousands of years before Darwin was one of evolution by trial and error? Imagine how much more there is which remains unproven but nevertheless valid and vital to our sense of meaning. The poetry, the myths and the legends of our past not only stir our imagination but also, it would appear, we cannot live without them.

To rediscover ourselves in Nature, we are going to need a new myth, or perhaps the redressing of an old one to help us. We need to reshape the way we think and speak about ourselves, about our history and about our relationship with the Earth. But where to look? I would like to recommend that we look in two directions, one to Africa itself and to the image and legend of one of her great trees, the *Ziziphus mucronata*, and the other to ancient Greece and to the great mythological oracle at Delphi – Apollo. Choose which one you prefer. I will show that they share the same message, that they are urgent and that their admonitions are the script for an intelligence that is ecological.

Central to the folklore of the Nguni people of southern Africa is the *Ziziphus mucronata*. They call it the tree of life. At any time in the year you will find on this tree a combination of green, yellow and brown leaves – the phases of youth, adulthood and old age. It is a hardy tree. In times of drought when grazing and browsing is scarce, the leaves on this tree remain resiliently intact. Its nutritionally rich foliage becomes the emergency food for antelopes and elephants as well as for humans, who mix the leaf pulp with water as a thirst-quencher. In hard times, even lions have been seen browsing upon its leaves.

A striking feature of the ziziphus is its thorns. Appearing as a double row, they are spaced along the length of every branch in pairs, each thorn directly opposite the other. But it is the shape of the paired thorns that is intriguing. One of the pair points robustly outward and forward while the other curves back and inwards in the opposite direction. The

Nguni legend says the thorns tell us something about ourselves – that we must look ahead, to the future ... but we must never forget where we have come from.

In the image of the backward-hooking thorn of the ziziphus, is the explanation of the Human-Nature split – we have forgotten our animal past. It is therefore the direction of our healing. By all means look ahead, keep moving, follow your dreams, but never forget your roots. Together the thorns say yes and no. They are poetic. One row points towards the future and to what we might become, the other towards the Earth and our origins. They represent the push of the human spirit on the one hand, the pull of soul on the other, the wings of psychology in one direction, the roots of our biology in the other. They are complementary opposites. They hold the tension between science and non-science, between subject and object, and it is crucial that we hold that tension, for within it is the definition of an ecological intelligence.

And then there is Apollo, the great mythological oracle of Ancient Greece. Apollo was the Homeric god of prophecy, medicine and culture – the embodiment of the poet, the naturalist and the scientist in all of us. His twin sister was the fabulous goddess of the wild, Artemis. Separate, yet inseparable, they anticipated each other. Apollo proposed three fundamental requirements for rediscovering our place in Nature:

> Know thyself.
> Do no thing in excess.
> Honour the gods.

"Remember where you have come from," says the Nguni legend. "Know thyself," said Apollo.
"The thorns are paired ... keep the balance," says the African legend. "Do no thing in excess," said Apollo.
"Honour the ancestors," say the Nguni. "Honour the gods," said Apollo.

When examined carefully, it will become evident that these admonitions are not as easy to follow as they might look. For a start, there is a definite order to them. To know thyself comes first. It anticipates the other two. It is a prerequisite for a greater awareness of the dynamics of balance and excess and of the nature of the "gods" within oneself.

The first admonition, to know thyself, is the big one. It is to remember where we have come from. It is to deepen our awareness of human origins, of species interdependence and of the transient nature of all things. To live this admonition is not going to be easy and the reason for this is that we will have to confront our own nature first. "To confront human nature, is to confront the absurd," says the French writer and philosopher, Albert Camus. "It is to confirm that there is no sun without shadow, and that it is essential to know the night." In other words, to know ourselves will include owning up to the "dark" side of our nature – our mostly unexplored, mostly undesirable qualities of personal greed, jealousy, aggression, our propensity to kill and our power-play.

To know thyself is an ongoing task. Like the curved thorn of the ziziphus it continually turns us around, bringing us face to face with ourselves in the world. To know thyself is to understand our wild nature. The psychological instincts of the predator, the parasite and the scavenger are in our history and in our blood. They will not go away, which means there is no point in turning a blind eye to them. To know thyself implies a willingness to review our prejudices and our sometimes inappropriate belief systems. It is to discover that one's identity is not restricted to a personal ego but includes a sense of self that is both ancient and evolutionary. But first, we must understand what we mean by the ego. We must understand its strengths and its limitations.

Coined by Sigmund Freud to describe that part of our personality that corresponds most nearly to the perceived self, it is another name for one's *autobiographical* self – our conscious sense of "me". The big problem with the ego, because it is our most relied upon model of the self, is that it is heavily biased in favour of seeing ourselves as separate and distinct from the rest of the world. In other words, the rest of the world is "out there", or as the theologian Alan Watts puts it in his critique of the "skin-encapsulated ego", what is in here is "me" and what is out there is "not me". This of course has led to the widespread belief that our ego-reality is the only one there is. As we shall find in what follows, this is not the case at all.

It is important, however, that we do not underestimate the significance of the human ego. It is mostly portrayed in a negative light, but without it we cannot make sense of our world. Like the conductor of an orchestra, it has an orientating function, co-ordinating skills such as memory, perception and intellect, as well as acting as a point of reference as to who we are and what we might become. Not as strong and as encompassing of the world as we sometimes like to think it is, it is just as well that it has its denial-oriented defences, which we will consider later. The ego, then, is a fairly recently evolved and tenuous attribute of the human mind and to witness its "disintegration" – as I have done as a psychiatrist – is to witness the frightening process of psychosis, a condition in which the boundaries between thoughts, feelings, perceptions and intuitions begin to blur until they become indistinguishable from each other.

Without an ego, without that sense of "me", we lose our gifts of insight and reflection. This is why analytical psychotherapy can be so meaningful. Ultimately, it is geared to strengthening the ego, not by bolstering its defences but by making it *less* defensive. It is about helping the patient to become less resistant to self-examination. To know thyself, then, is a lifelong process of learning to see ourselves in the other, of seeing the world as a mirror and of being accountable for our personal contributions towards our own suffering.

The second admonition, to do no thing in excess … to keep the balance, is not merely a caution against addictions to foods, beverages and drugs. It is a caution against being obsessive about any one *thing* – a dream, a memory, a doctrine or a cause. It is to remember the other row of thorns on the branch of the ziziphus. Keep the focus but learn to scan as well. Importantly, this does not imply that sometimes boring notion of doing everything in moderation. Apollo did not say, "Do nothing in excess". The first admonition will already have alerted us to the fact that we are naturally immoderate, self-concerned and, given half a chance, pleasure-seeking. We want it all and we want it now. Have our excesses, Apollo implied, but do not find yourself addicted or obsessed by them. In other words, we must learn how and when to say yes and no to our preoccupations and to our extremes.

To honour the gods ... and the ancestors, is to honour the multiple expressions of the Earth, of the Universe, of Creation. It is more than an acknowledgement of respect for the human forefathers and mothers. It is an honouring of the unique intelligence in everything – the trees, the land, the sea, the animals, as well as people. It is to know what it means when the "bushman" hunter-gatherers of the Kalahari say that together all the creatures of the land say ONE thing – we are connected. It is to have a deep respect for life in all its forms and expressions and to know that even the land, when we are prepared to listen, knows how to say yes and no to us.

To honour the gods is to "think molecular". It is to appreciate the chemistry of survival at its simplest level, to be grateful for our genetically-primed drives to seek or explore, to find food and water, to socialise, to protect, provide and to procreate. It is to be unashamed of our needs to compete, to confront, to play and, when necessary, to run away. It is to take the experience of spirit and soul seriously. Listen to what D H Lawrence had to say about honouring the gods:

> That I am I.
> That my soul is a dark forest.
> That strange gods come forth
> From the forest into the clearing of
> My known self, and then go back.
> That I must have the courage to let
> Them come and go.

That I will never let mankind put
anything over me, but that I will
try always to recognize and to
honour the gods in me and the gods
in other men and women.

It is going to take a peculiar intelligence and a peculiar language to understand the consequences of what it means to live the admonitions of the ziziphus and of Apollo, including the consequences of not living them. It is what this book is about. It is an invitation to say yes to an intelligence that can reshape the myths of humanity; that can reshape our language of dissonance in favour of one that is at home at the Human-Nature interface; that continually reminds us that there are sometimes more important, yet less familiar ways of thinking about ourselves and of our relationship to the world. It is a language which, in the words of the Irish poet Seamus Heaney, "because of its profound representation of the process of discovering things in the world would be bound to be poetry".

The word poetry has its roots in the Latin and Greek words *poeme* and *poema*, meaning to create or make. It can be seen as the art of rhythmical composition, written or spoken, or as a way of exacting pleasure by beautiful, imaginative or elevated thoughts. However, it is important that we do not confine poetry to that which is refined and sentimental. Poetry does not always exact pleasure or beauty in the way we expect it to, for it can be both bloody and bloodless. It sees the wild face of beauty too – the violent beauty of a wild-dog "kill", for instance, or the stark sight of a grove of fallen trees pushed over by elephants. And we all have something of the poet in us. Absurd? Not at all, for we all know, even in a small way, what it means to say yes to the world and then no ... and then yes again. It is our first language.

To be sensitive to the cadence of yes and no is to remember that between you and me, between you and an elephant, a heron, a river or a tree, there is a space that has to be respected and which, at times, we ignore at our peril. Poetry is the only language I know capable of effectively describing that space and as we shall see, it is part of the necessary task of asking permission to enter that space. Sometimes you are permitted to enter into it and sometimes you are not. Poetry is therefore more than a language. It is an attitude and if we've forgotten it, it is our task to remember it again. We urgently need tongues that can speak with care, anger, protest – not the scattered or whinging prose of the fanatic – but the voice of those who can speak of anger and beauty in the same breath. Only poetry can do this. It is a language of protest but it is also a language of hope.

Poetry, then, because it is unafraid of what is raw, because it is rooted, because it reaches out and hooks back at the same time, because it outlives us and because all other art forms are a form of poetry, is the obvious language for an ecological intelligence. Put another way, it is difficult to find another language that can better describe the way a lion walks or how a fish eagle swoops to scoop its prey. How else can we describe the sound of the wind through the reeds or the changing colours of the clouds in a western sky if not poetically? How can we better communicate the first breath of a child, the dying breath of an elephant or the sloppy death of thirty or more Roan antelope in transit to a foreign country, if not through the rawness of poetry?

When we no longer shudder at the ecological warning calls of science, it would seem that the only voice left that can awaken us belongs to the poets. Poetry comes at us from both sides, from inside and from out. It will not let us off the hook and if we listen to the language carefully, it should not take long to understand that it is the language of soul. We have to be able to shudder.

If you are with me, you will understand that the poetry I am interested in is not necessarily that of verse and rhyme. I am interested in the lines and images that are felt in the bones of the reader, that make children ask for a second reading and that stir the exhausted mindsets of civil servants who can't wait until they retire. I am interested in the poems that unite the scientist and the artist in us – the poems that can

hold the tension and the wisdom between the words yes a
welcome the poetry that says "No!" to what we are doing to tne ianu anu
the sea; "Yes!" to those that speak for our healing. Let's welcome the
poetry that reminds us of our "creatureliness", as Heaney puts it – the
ones that rhyme with our history. Through the guidance of poetry, let's
take that clumsy yet essential first step towards rediscovering ourselves
in Nature. The choice is ours, says the poet, Rilke:

> Wherever you are:
> tonight I want you
> to take one step
> out of your house ...

Read this poem by Antonio Machado aloud. And then, please, read it
again. Its title is its first five words:

> The wind, one brilliant day, called
> to my soul with an odor of jasmine.
>
> "In return for the odor of my jasmine,
> I'd like all the odor of your roses"
>
> "I have no roses; all the flowers
> in my garden are dead."
>
> "Well then, I'll take the withered petals
> and the yellow leaves and the waters of the fountain."
>
> The wind left. And I wept. And my soul said to me:
> "What have you done with the garden that was entrusted to you?"

When Machado asks, *what have you done with the garden?* ... we know
exactly who he is addressing. He is speaking to you and me. When Rilke
says: *tonight I want you to step out of your house*, we know exactly what

he means. Tonight I want you to think and to speak about the world and the wild, differently.

Unlike Shakespeare's definition of love that alters not as it alteration finds, poetry alters as it alteration finds. Poetry is not unconditional. And yet, like love, it too endures. It has a life of its own, it is elusive. It refuses, like spirit and soul, to be measured. It is random yet ever present. As the Mexican poet and Nobel laureate Octavio Paz says, " ... it slips between yes and no ... it is real ... And as soon as I say IT IS REAL, it vanishes. It is not speech. It is an act."

Ecological intelligence is not speech. It is an act. It is an act of weaving and unweaving our reflections of ourselves on Earth, of scattering eyes upon it and of scattering the Earth upon our eyes. It comes alive between yes and no, between what is and what is not, between science and non-science. And as soon as it becomes acquisitive, something egotistic ... it vanishes.

Some will say that these are the lamentations of a romantic and I will answer yes ... and no. I am a romantic, as well as an occasional stray idealist, but not in a sentimental sense. I do not believe in utopias. Instead, let me remind you, in the words of the South African poet Stephen Watson, what it means to be a romantic in the great traditional sense of the word: "It was and is, rather, one expression of a perennial human tendency to protest against that which would confine and otherwise mutilate what used to be called the human soul." He tells us that to be a romantic is not only to be someone who expects adventure around every corner, but who is capable of "placing oneself in that long Romantic tradition of protest against a mechanised and (sometimes) heartless world."

Does this mean that the romantic is anti-mechanisation and, in the same vein, anti-science? Far from it. One of the main concerns of this book is to remind the reader of the common ground between the scientist and the poet. It is an attempt to acknowledge, as the socio-biologist E O Wilson and the philosopher Karl Popper affirm, that the poet and the scientist draw from the same unconscious reservoir of myths and images. They share the same boldness of imagination. They both concern themselves with discovering and communicating natural laws in a language marked by elegance – a beautiful word for the right mix of simplicity, clarity and latent power. Where the two differ, however, as we shall see, is in their methodology. Scientists, says Wilson, aim for a generalising formula to which special cases are obedient, seeking unifying natural laws, while poets "invent special cases immediately". To me, the scientist says, "Let's go out and prove it." The poet says, "Let's go out and disprove it." Where the poet and the scientist stand united, however, is in the essence of their work. Wilson puts it this way: "Their works are lit by a personal flame and above all else, they are committed to the abstract ideal of truth in the midst of clamouring demands of ego and ideology. They pass the acid test of promoting new knowledge even at the expense of losing credit for it. In a sense, science and poetry are not professions – they are vocations." They are vocations committed to new ways of seeing things and of saying them.

In 1952, the French poet Francis Ponge published an essay on poetry called "The Silent World Is Our Only Homeland." In it, he describes the process and function of poetry:

> It is to nourish the spirit of man by giving him the cosmos to suckle. We have only to lower our standard of dominating nature and to raise our standards of participating in it in order to make the reconciliation take place. When man becomes proud to be not just the site where ideas and feelings are produced, but also the crossroad where they divide and mingle, he will be ready to be saved. Hope therefore lies in a poetry through which the world so invades the spirit of man, that he becomes almost speechless, and later re-invents a language. Poets are the ambassadors of the silent world. As such, they stammer, they murmur, they sink into the darkness of logos – until at last they reach the level of ROOTS, where things and formulae are one. This is why, whatever one says, poetry is much

more important than any other art, any other science. This is also why poetry has nothing in common with the poetry anthologies of today. True poetry is what does not pretend to be poetry. It is in the dogged drafts of a few maniacs seeking the new encounter.

If we are to begin to rediscover ourselves in Nature, let's begin to live the ecological intelligence that we seek ... little by little. If a poetic encounter with the world and, in this case, with ourselves, is going to be a dogged one and if it is going to be up to a few maniacs like you and me to undertake it, then let's do it. Let's look at the root meaning of the word "enthusiasm" and live it, literally. It comes from the Greek *enthousiasmos*, which means "to be filled with the gods". Let's remember where we have come from.

*Nothing in biology makes sense except
in the light of evolution.*

Theodosius Dobzhansky (1973)

Ye are the salt of the earth.

St Matthew

2

EVOLUTION IN PERSPECTIVE

"WHERE WERE YOU WHEN I LAID THE FOUNDATIONS OF THE EARTH?" IS the famous question asked by the Old Testament God of Job after he had complained to his maker about his miserable fate. Not surprisingly, the response was one of silence. How would you have answered that one? I think your silence would have been as loud as mine.

"Where were you?" I believe this to be a personal question and a profoundly evolutionary one. It as a question that demands an ecological answer. Perhaps, by reviewing our remarkable history, we might discover that we are a lot closer to those foundations than we previously imagined.

THE KNOWN AND THE UNKNOWN UNIVERSE

The known universe, according to recent estimates, is somewhere between thirteen and fifteen billion years old – fifteen thousand million years! How did it all begin? Well, we don't really know. General consensus acknowledges a Big Bang as the starting point, not only of the explosive outward trek of radiation, particles, molecules, gas and dust – all of these constellating over millions of years into the supernovas, galaxies, stars and planets that we call the Cosmos – but of the beginning of Time. It is indeed a conundrum, a situation begging the question: "What happened before the 'big' event?" Once again, we don't really know. Instead, our imaginations are now being stirred by a host of new hotly debated theories about alternative or parallel universes to ours, including notions of multiple conditions of existence outside our usual, three dimensional one, some of them having little to do with the timing of the Big Bang. As they say, watch this space.

While no one knows what happened before the Big Bang, we think we know what happened directly afterwards. In that first trillionth of a second, gravity and the four dimensions of length, breadth, height and time were born. For the time being, let's stay with the universe we know, or at least, the one that we pretend to know. What does it consist of?

The visible matter, from planets, stars, galaxies and nebulae etc ... everything that the eye can see, telescopes and all, is believed to be a tiny one percent of what we know (it could be even less). Ninety-nine percent of the universe, then, is invisible! About three percent of what is invisible is made up of baryonic matter (protons, neutrons and electrons), intergalactic gas, brown dwarfs and black holes (a gravitational force so powerful that neither light, protons, neutrons and atoms can escape). A further twenty-three percent is made up of another kind of dark matter in the form of exotic, unknown particles. We don't know what they are but we know that they are there. If this sounds absurd then what about the remaining seventy percent of our outwardly-accelerating universe? Simply referred to as dark energy, it is believed to be the cosmic force responsible for the acceleration of the galaxies, some of them at speeds faster than the speed of light. Akin to Einstein's notion of antigravity – what he once called his "biggest blunder". – this force is yet to be positively identified, but we know it is there.

In an interesting parallel, it is estimated that seventy percent of the world's living species, from bacteria to worms, ants, flowering plants, mammals and even primates, have yet to be identified. Forget about space, we hardly know what's on our own doorstep. And if you don't mind a poetic parallel, we might as well be saying the same thing for how little we know about the human mind, itself a phenomenon in process – exotic, precious and with its own blind spots and black holes, its own dark energy and its own peculiar resistance to gravity.

Looking around us, we appear to be alone. We are uncertain. We think we know *where* we are but the answer as to the *why* is not readily forthcoming. *What* we are, as we shall see, is easy. We are human animals –

curious, witty, aggressive, reflective, wonderful and pathetic and, as Anthony Fairall of the Department of Astronomy at the University of Cape Town once quipped, "this is the right time for us to be here".

COSMIC TIME

So, this is our time and this is where we are: Earth. We are biologically in it and of it, children of a 4.5 billion-year-old planet and a 5.5 billion-year-old star called the Sun. Rotating around our parental star in a 365-day solar year, we are part of a tiny solar system in an equally tiny corner of a trillion-star cluster known as the Milky Way Galaxy. At the centre of our galaxy is a black hole around which our solar system and the rest of the Milky Way spins. This dark and massive force, when viewed from Earth, is somewhere beyond the constellation of Sagittarius, about forty-thousand light-years away. That's how long, in years, it will take us to get there if we were travelling at 300,000 kilometres per second – the speed of light. It is indeed, in human dimensions, a long, long way from home.

While these figures might be comprehensible to some, they are meaningless, really, unless we can bring them down to Earth, so to speak. By referring to cosmic years, the eminent British astronomer, Sir Patrick Moore, has given us a way of condensing our notion of time to a more user-friendly scale.

A cosmic year is the equivalent of 225 million solar years – the time it takes for our solar system to rotate once around the center our galaxy. This tells us that if the Earth is 4.5 billion solar years old, then in cosmic years, dividing 4.5 billion by 225 million, the Earth is twenty cosmic years old. The Earth, then, has circled the black hole centre of our galaxy roughly twenty times in its history. To put a human life span onto this time scale, three-score-and-ten years translates into roughly nine cosmic seconds. And so, using the model of cosmic time, let's review our evolutionary milestones. See how this compares with conventional time in the following diagram:

GEOLOGICAL TIME-SCALE

10 'seconds' = 70 years
2 'hours' = 40 000 years
↓

'COSMIC' TIME	AGE IN MILLIONS OF YEARS	EPOCHS / GEOLOGICAL SYSTEMS Maximum thickness in metres	TIME-RANGES OF LIFE GROUPS
1,7 'days'	1 —		
	15 —	PLIOCENE 5 500 m	
1 'month'		MIOCENE 6 400 m	
2 'months'	35 —		
	45 —	OLIGOCENE 4 500 m	
3 'months'	75 —	EOCENE 7 000 m	
6 'months'		CRETACEOUS 19 500 m	
7 'months'	140 —		
8 'months'	170 —	JURASSIC 6 700 m	
9 'months'	195 —	TRIASSIC 7 500 m	
1 'year'	220 —	PERMIAN 5 500 m	
	275 —	CARBONIFEROUS 12 000 m	
	320 —	DEVONIAN 11 300 m	
	350 —	SILURIAN 6 100 m	
1,5 'years'	420 —	ORDOVICIAN 12 000 m	
2 'years'	520 —	CAMBRIAN 12 000 m	
9 'years'	2000 —	PRE-CAMBRIAN Unknown thickness	

Geological eras (vertical): TERTIARY, MESOZOIC, PALAEOZOIC, ARCHAEN

Time-ranges of life groups (vertical labels): →SEAWEEDS AND INVERTEBRATE ANIMALS, ↑LAND PLANTS, →FISHES, →AMPHIBIA, →REPTILES, →BIRDS, →MAMMALS, →MAN

↑
20 'years' = 4.5 billion solar years

The first two "years" of the Earth's existence was one of molten fury – a fiery hangover from its split from the sun. Unable to generate its own heat, it began to cool and about 18 cosmic years ago our hot pre-Cambrian planet – so-named after the rocks of Cambria, the former name of present day Wales – gave rise to the world's oldest known igneous rocks. These molten elements solidified into the well-known crystal shapes of ancient granite and basalt. With the cooling of the Earth came the ocean-forming rains and the beginning of a geological process called the cycle of stones. The alternating heat and cold of day and night caused the rocks to swell and to retract until, exhausted by the process, the outer geological skin of the basalts and granites began to erode and flake off. Carried away by wind and water, it took another two cosmic years for the first great rock formations to erode their way to the seas. The first stage in the cycle was over.

Under the massive weight of oxygen-free water, the second stage of the cycle began. In a process of geological transformation, layer upon layer of the exfoliated and eroded igneous tissue compressed to become the oldest known sedimentary rocks on Earth. The crystals in these strata, under intense heat and pressure, were transformed in the third stage into the tough, elegantly grained metamorphic form that we find in the present-day mountain ranges such as the Alps and the Himalayas.

As a metaphor for the shaping of human life and character, it would appear that our personal fine and coarse-grained life experiences, our patterns of weathering, trauma and transformations are not unlike those patterns in the cycle of stones. Meanwhile, it is curious to think, as the British geologist and archaeologist Jaquetta Hawkes puts it, that

> ... granite and basalt, with water, nitrogen and carbon dioxide in combination with the early atmosphere of Earth, have made all the material paraphernalia with which man now surrounds himself, the sky-scraper, the wine glass, the vacuum cleaner, jewels, the mirror into which I look. And the woman who looks? Where did it

come from, this being behind the eyes, this thing that asks? How has this been gleaned from a landscape of harsh rock and empty seas?

It would seem that we cannot escape our molecular and geological foundations. They are in our blood.

ORGANIC LIFE

With the unravelling of DNA sequences in living forms, most biologists now acknowledge three Domains of life. These are the Bacteria – the conventional microbes of the world; the Archae, ancient single-cell, organisms that inhabit environments of extreme temperature and acidity (thermacidophiles), salty environments (halobacteria) and anoxic bogs (methanogenic bacteria). The third domain comprises the Eukarya – organisms that are made up of cells with organelles and a separate, membrane-bound nucleus. The Eukarya comprise the fungi, the plants and all animals including us.

The Archae were the first organic inhabitants of the Earth. Without them, there would be no trees, flowers or fish ... and we wouldn't be here either. But when and how did they come about? As for the when, we believe it to be about thirteen or fourteen cosmic years ago (three billion years). The how is speculative but highly likely. With sixty percent of the granites already established, the electro-chemical mixture of land, water and lightning combined to produce molecular compounds of nitrogen, carbon and other elements that had not existed on Earth before. There was no turning back. A process had been initiated in which the electrically-charged molecules combined to form water-borne organisms capable of living in an oxygen-free world. The next step in the process was crucial: the development of a membrane – the first organic boundary, the first fence, the first hint of specialisation.

However, if there was ever a defining moment in the evolution of life as we know it, it occurred about ten cosmic years (about two billion years) ago. It marks the earliest evidence of one of the great strategies of species survival: symbiosis – so named by the German botanist Anton de Bary in 1873 to describe the living together of different organisms for mutual benefit. With it came the emergence of the first differentiated cells. These were the first cells to have organelles and a nucleus with its own membrane. The reason for the nuclear membrane will become clear. But what triggered this first symbiotic relationship? It was the changing conditions of the surroundings.

In an environment that was becoming increasingly oxygenated, new aerobic (oxygen-coping) bacteria began to emerge, putting them at a clear advantage over the anaerobes. With competition for nutrients becoming increasingly serious, including a phase when, in all likelihood, the two strains of bacteria were feeding off each other, the first great alliance took place. Instead of being devoured by the predatory anaerobes, the more recent, thread-like aerobic organisms became part of the intra-cellular structure of their evolutionary older anaerobic cousins. They literally came on board, where they function to this day, in all living cells, as the indispensable organelles responsible for the conversion of oxygen into energy. Essential for cellular metabolism and homeostasis, these little sub-compartments of our cells are known as the mitochondria, from the Greek *mitos*, meaning thread, and *chondrion*, meaning granule. Because of the energy they generate, they are also called the "powerhouses" of the cells. Without them we would not be able to move, think or dream. Without them, the animal and insect kingdoms as we know them today would not exist.

The symbiotic relationship, however, was a "conditional" one. The host cells, compelled to protect their own DNA, ensured their long-term survival by developing a membrane around their nuclei. The mitochondria, for the same reason, developed a double membrane. This genetic independence of the cell nuclei and mitochondria brings a fascinating twist to the symbiotic tale. It is well known that the genetic information in the nucleus of mammalian cells comes from both parents. What we didn't know until very recently is that the genetic information in the mitochondria, generation after generation, is passed on by the female of the species only. In other words, the mitochondria, the powerhouses of our cells, come from our biological mothers. Why there is no contribution from the biological father is unknown, but it would seem that the genetic information, if any, which the sperm may carry regarding the mitochondria is either absent or, if not, lost or destroyed at the moment of conception. Be that as it may, the maternal link to our mitochondria has opened up a fascinating avenue into our understanding of human ancestry. With the discovery of this lineage, we are able to show that modern humans, *Homo sapiens sapiens*, as little as 200,000 years ago shared not only a common blood-line, but as recently as sixty-thousand years ago, a lineage through six or seven possible biological mothers. As humans, it would seem that we are more closely related to each other than we sometimes like to think. As for our link with animals, the evidence suggests that the mammalian bloodline goes back 100 million years. It would appear that the poetry of the brotherhood and sisterhood of all living things has become science.

A similar symbiotic process occurred in plant cells as well but where the new bacterial tenants (cyanobacteria) are what are known as chloroplasts – the "green stuff" of plants. Instead of using oxygen, they combine carbon dioxide with water and light to produce oxygen. As it is with mitochondria, chloroplasts too, have their own DNA.

It should therefore not be surprising to learn that other biological partnerships followed. One of the most important of these partnerships is described by the science-writers John Briggs and F David Peat in their book *Turbulent Mirror* as "the taking into the cell in another intrusion-turned-marriage the highly mobile, cork-screw shaped bacteria" – the spirochetes. Once again, in return for nourishment and protection, the spirochetes, or "wrigglers", as neuroscientist and author Lynn Margulis calls them, made their sluggish hosts an offer they couldn't refuse. They brought with them their stout cilia, or hair-like propelling strands, to act as miniature outboard motors for their new hosts. Could this have been a hint of the future legs and wings to come? Perhaps so, but not all "wrigglers" became propelling mechanisms. Some of them developed into micro-tubules within the host cell, eventually joining and elongating to become what is believed to be primitive axons and dendrites – the "business ends" of neurones as Margulis describes them. As she suggests, it is not improbable that the growing network of connecting tubules developed into neurological tissue and later, much later, the first brains.

Moving on to four cosmic years ago (nine hundred million years), we would have found ourselves in the company of the planet's first multicellular plants. Known as stromatolites from the Greek *stroma*, meaning matrix or tissue, they established themselves in networks of algae or algal beds. One galactic-turn later we would have seen the first jellyfish, coelenterata, and only two cosmic years ago, the trilobites – the world's first insects. Marine and land invertebrates were developing their first shells, or exoskeletons, and then came the glaciation of an African landmass very different to its modern shape. With the receding of the ice roughly 1.5 cosmic years ago the sea became home to horn corals and boneless fish – the predecessors of modern sharks.

With a steady increase in temperatures, the Earth produced its first tree ferns, sharks and early amphibians. The stage was set for what seemed to be an inevitable explosion of life, but it was not to be. Instead, as a result of large-scale volcanic activity and global warming, carbon dioxide levels rose to toxic proportions, wiping out ninety-five percent of the Earth's species! This catastrophic occurrence, a fraction more than one cosmic year ago and now referred to as the Permian Extinction, heralded a new geological period on our planet – the Triassic. The survivors regrouped themselves. New forms began to take shape, among them the ancestors of modern turtles, sharks and the much-maligned crocodile, surely the greatest survivors of all modern animals. Gymnosperms (our non-flowering trees and plants) began to carpet many parts of the world, contributing not only to an increase in the Earth's atmospheric oxygen, but to a change in the weather too. Increasing forestation meant increasing rainfall. The rivers began to flow freely, providing a niche for countless riverine plants, fish and insects. Nine "months" (180 million years) ago, in a new period known as the Jurassic, the dinosaurs (from the

Greek words *deinos*, meaning terrible, and *sauros*, meaning lizard), became the food-chain champions of the world.

A "month" later, accompanied by a splash of colours, plants with sexual organs made their first appearance. The flowers of the fields opened their petals and sepals to expose stamens and pistils – the respective male (pollen producing) and female (seed producing) components of flowers. Drawn to the plethora of colours and perfumes came an equal plethora of unwitting pollinators in the forms of wasps, flies, butterflies and bees.

Spiders and crustaceans introduced themselves to the Earth's ecosystems at about the same time as the flowering plants, while behind the scenes, a group of dinosaurs (they weren't all as big as *Tyrannosaurus rex*) evolved a new way of escaping their larger, hungry relatives: their scales softened into feathers. Examine a reptilian scale through a powerful microscope and you would discover that its molecular architecture is practically identical to that of a feather. And so it was, only seven "months" (about 130 million years) ago that *Archaeopteryx*, the first known feathered creature (with teeth!) – a true ancestor of the birds – took to the sky. Escaping predators was a huge benefit to the feathered creatures, but there were other advantages as well: flight provided new and wonderful opportunities for insulation, feeding, nesting and travel.

At the same time as the birds (now warm-blooded) began taking flight, the Earth's surface began to split up again. It was the start of a significant land migration, otherwise known as continental drift. This major break-up and spread of the southerly landmass took about four cosmic months (seventy million years) to give us the recognisable continents of South America, Africa, Antarctica and Australia as well as the subcontinent of India. The Earth's anatomy, like a huge geological embryo, had, in a sense, differentiated itself.

Need we be reminded that the same pattern of anatomical differentiation occurs in every living embryo, from stem cells to livers, kidneys, hearts, spleens and brains? Is global anatomy a metaphor worth taking seriously? Can we learn from our own bodies? To me, the human anatomy is one of the finest examples I know of biological differentiation and diversity. It is a living definition of ecology, an embodiment of the interactions and interdependence between molecules, cells, tissues, organs and systems, sensitive to both inner and outer environments. Sociologically it would appear to be the same – we are a body of humans, drifting and differentiated at the same time, interacting and relating to each other and we do it because we have to. As we shall see, it is part of our survival as bio-psycho-social beings.

A little over three cosmic months ago (sixty-five million years), not too long before the establishment of the continents as we know them today, the dinosaur's dominant reign ended. It is chillingly specu-lated that the cause of this abrupt ending to the dinosaurs' 120 million-year existence was a massive asteroid impact on the Yucatan peninsula of present day northern Mexico. It is thought that the event caused so much dust to be thrown into the atmosphere that the sun all but disappeared from the sky. The resulting drop in temperature was so severe that the sun-dependent creatures stood no chance of survival.

How do we know that this theory is the correct one? Well, we don't know for sure, but it seems to be the most likely one. What we do know is that there was indeed an asteroid impact as described. The element Iridium is the signature of asteroid impacts and there is plenty of it in a huge but well-defined area on the Yucatan peninsula. It is dated to sixty-five million years ago. We also know that the dinosaurs made their surprisingly rapid exit at about that time. As plausible as they might seem, the evidence for at least two contending theories – a decimating epidemic or an intolerable atmospheric/climatic change of another kind – has not been substantiated. Of the three possibilities for extinc-tion, which one could the human animal be facing?

And so, in what could be described as a huge coincidence, the demise of the dinosaurs gave the burrowing, warm-blooded placentals, Class Mammalia, the opportunity to establish themselves. While this is our class, there were no mammalian forms at that time even vaguely ready to put up their hands, or wiggle their thumbs. The geological period known as the Cretaceous, from the Latin word for chalk, had ended and a warm-blooded class of creatures tentatively tip-toed into the Tertiary. The burrowing lemurs, shrews, rats and mice showed their day-time faces. Ancestral ungulates and other ancient carnivores announced themselves, along with a fresh spurt of newly evolving birds, insects, frogs, worms, mosses and new flowering plants.

AFRICAN ORIGINS

About two cosmic months ago the Great Rift Valley began to open up and, peering into it and out of it, were the tiny evolutionary cousins of the elephant, the Family Procaviidae – the hyraxes of bush, trees and rocks. The aardvark and the early rhino made their acquaintance with Africa about one "month" ago. Then, with the world wide expansion of grasslands only twelve cosmic days later, the hollow-horned antelopes showed up alongside their slightly older ruminant companions, the giraffes, with their horns of solid bone. Bulk-feeders such as the buffalo, *Syncerus caffer*, began herding themselves out of Europe and into the African grasslands while the zebra (family Equidae), whose ancestors hail from South America, declared their savannah stripes. As if to balance the wilderness equation, the modern carnivores such as the lion and the hyena, left their European origins to become part of the African food chain. This all took place about six "days" (three to four million years) ago.

Twenty-four cosmic hours later, not far from the foothills of the newly-formed volcanic slopes of Kilimanjaro, an astonishingly odd-looking primate stood up. It was an ape-like being of the genus *Australopithecus* (from the Latin *australis*, meaning southern and the Greek *pithekos*, meaning ape). Genetically different to the hominids that are linked to modern orang-utans, these bipedal creatures of the sub-family homininae, now extinct, are our earliest hominin ancestors.

There appears to be little doubt about who our early ancestors are but what is unclear is our ancestry – the line of descent. From

Australopithecus to modern man, what we do know, however, is that the progressive increases in brain size of our intermediate ancestors and, with it, a consciousness that would eventually define the human animal, has the quality of quantum leaps. The diminishing gaps in time between the increments has forced us to revise our notions of evolution as something slow and purposive. Let's have a look at these leaps.

With a brain size of 750cc, *Homo habilis*, our original hominin grandparents, appeared on Earth about four cosmic days ago (2,5 million years). It would appear that they lived in an overlap phase with their smaller-brained but similar looking cousins, *Australopithecus africanus* and *bosei*. One animal among many others alongside our Australopithecan cousins must have been watching the early development of the hominin family. It was the African elephant, *Loxodonta africana*, who emerged from their own ancestral line at more or less the same time as *Homo habilis*, the world's first toolmakers. *Habilis*, from the Latin *habilis*, meaning dextrous, is linked with the first discovery of concentrations of animal remains, as well as stone collections, many of which had been brought from long distances. These "pebble tools", "choppers" and water-worn cobbles crudely flaked on one side to form a jagged cutting edge, were mankind's first embellished stone tools.

Habilis, apart from having a wider range of equipment, also had a different arrangement of teeth to those of their Australopithecan relatives. They were, indeed, a different species. The back teeth of these toolmaking hominins were narrower, suggesting the development of an important change in their diets – they were eating more animal food than their mostly-vegetarian ancestors. As for the size of the *habilis* brain, not only was it larger than that of Australopithecus, but, for the first time, the bulge of Broca's area, the convolution of the brain corresponding to the centre for executive speech, became evident on a primate skull.

In their book *The Wisdom of Bones*, Alan Walker and Pat Shipman remind us that the anatomical capacity for speech is also a reflection of other particular mental abilities including the ability to categorize and analyse the world in a complex fashion. It includes the capacity to name and to talk *about* things, as well as to describe actions without performing them. The Earth had a new tongue. Our early hominin grandparents were not only the carriers of stones and bones, they were also the carriers and shapers of words.

About one-and-a-half cosmic days ago (a million years), Africa was witness to another sudden leap in the size of the hominin skull. *Homo erectus* emerged with a 1200–1300cc brain. Also known as *Homo ergaster*, or "The Work Man", these ancestors brought with them an up-to-date tool kit containing a variety of large symmetrically-flaked stone bifaces, or hand axes, for chopping, cutting, piercing and pounding. They, too, were anatomically different to their immediate ancestors. Compared with *habilis*, the faces of *erectus* had become smaller as well as more expressive, while their evenly spaced and smaller back teeth confirmed the early shift from a primarily vegetable diet to one that included significantly more animal protein. This increase in brain size was believed to be a reflection of the cognitive requirements for co-operative hunting and living as well as for the evolutionary significant gift of story telling and symbol formation. It was also associated with the capacity to harness that great element of the gods – fire.

Fire meant an extension of the light into the night. It became a gravitational force, gathering people around it not only for warmth and safety, but for story telling. The dark became less frightening. Essential for the developing brains of the hominins to come, cellulose-rich plants could be cooked and transformed into energy providing carbohydrates. With fire we were able to keep pantries and to establish ourselves in previously formidable geographical areas. Fired by the exploratory flames of human consciousness, we zigzagged our way out of Africa into south-eastern and eastern Asia, a poetic, yet cognitive, equivalent of continental drift.

About eight cosmic hours ago (250,000 years), a hominin with a 1450cc brain showed up. It was the grand entrance of *Homo sapiens*, from the Latin word *sapia*, which means "wise". These large-brain ancestors did not include our heavily browed, hairy and more muscled cousin, *Homo neanderthalensis*. Matthias Krings of the University of Munich has shown that there is a significant difference between the DNA of Neanderthal Man and that of modern human beings, which means, although related to us, they were altogether a different species. It is not known exactly when our Neanderthal relatives became extinct (estimates are between fifty-thousand and 200 000 years ago), but, in spite of ten thousand years of living side by side with *H. sapiens* in Europe and the Middle East, we think we know why. It is believed they were vanquished by none other than their highly inventive and aggressive hominin cousins – us.

The next step in our evolution has to be regarded as one of the great cognitive milestones in our history – the beginnings of sophisticated art. Prior to as little as forty-thousand years ago no rock art or engravings of any aesthetic significance, whether on bone or stone, are known to exist. It is as if from one level of capability to another, human creativity took a quantum leap. The signature and skill of an artist hitherto unknown suddenly emerged. The great sand faces of the Earth became the diaries of human experience as well as the mirrors of the human soul. Modern man had arrived.

So this is who we are – *Homo sapiens sapiens* – the sole survivors of at least eighteen species of bipedal ancestors. We are privileged. Creative and clever? Yes. Doubly wise? I doubt it.

CULTURAL EVOLUTION

The human animal travelled the world. Equipped with a brain that was primed to seek and to explore, we had no choice. The search for food and new hunting grounds made sure of that until, close on the heels of the last ice age 10,000 years ago and with the Earth's temperatures warming again, one of Nature's most fortuitous genetic accidents occurred. It stopped our nomadic ancestors in their tracks. By some great fluke, or perhaps the result of a hitherto unknown, temperature-dependent bacterial alliance with wild grasses, a wind-scattered, wild wheat with fourteen chromosomes crossed with a natural goat grass of the same chromosome number. The result was a fertile twenty-eight-chromosome hybrid called "emmer". The seeds of this edible hybrid were still light enough to be wind borne but then a second accident occurred when "emmer" crossed with another goat grass, producing a still larger hybrid with forty-two chromosomes. This hybrid is the cereal called bread wheat, *Triticum vulgare*, the staple diet of millions of people today.

Prior to this, the order of the day was to collect grass seeds and to bring them home, but suddenly, in an exotic, symbiotic relationship beautifully described by the scientist and philosopher J Bronowski, "man and a plant came together". A grain had developed that was too heavy for wind-dispersal and which had to be cultivated by a species that understood the behaviour of flowering plants and grasses. By accident or coincidence, the coalition of natural grasses to form cereals accelerated. Barley, *Hordeum vulgare*, sprang up in the Middle East, followed by maize, *Zea mays*, in the American tropics 7000 years ago. Nearly two thousand years later, rice, *Oryza sativa*, cropped up in Thailand and China, while in Africa sorghum, *Sorghum bicolour*, and the millets, *Pennisetum glaucum*, and *Eleusine corocana*, began seeding themselves. At last, the hominins were able to take off their nomadic shoes and stay put for a while. Planting, cultivating, harvesting and the domesticating and interbreeding of animals signalled another quantum jump in the evolution of human culture. It added a dimension to the definition of home. It gave us the time and the luxury to reflect upon matters beyond our immediate survival. It was the beginning of surplus and of specialisation, a time not only to tell tales, but to embellish them. Personal lives became stories, stories became legends, legends became myths and our myths became our dreams.

If the traditional agricultural practices of Africa, India and the Far East are anything to go by, it should not surprise us to learn that women were the first agriculturists. Who else would have intuited better the significance of fertility, pregnancy and cultivation? Who other than the traditional gatherers of the plains would have recognised the potential of a new food source when it presented itself?

Agriculture has been important in our history but it came with a price. Cultivation is synonymous with growth and therein lies the shadow or the dark side of this evolutionary event. It is called expansionism. Staying in one place led to an unprecedented growth in local populations. This meant a need for more food. More food meant competition for more land and it is not difficult to see the link between land, territory, colonisation and the means of getting it – politics and war. Cultivation took on a new dimension – the cultivation of words, wealth and weapons.

There was no turning back, but it had its positive side. Human language took on another form. Through exquisite, painstaking art, including our earliest scribbled signs and symbols, our agricultural ancestors wrote themselves into the record book. No longer restricted to body signals and to speech, language in its written form allowed the human animal to record, to think in words and to read between the lines. From rock faces to papyrus and paper, the files of human history became indelible and, as every poet will tell you, ink and blood are the same thing.

With the onset of agriculture and the interweaving seasons of bread and wine, cultivation became a multifaceted metaphor for the human narrative – the seasons of birth, death and rebirth. It reinforced in us the Neanderthal notion of continuity and an after-life, for these relatives were the first hominins to add to the graves of their dead something for an afterlife – flowers, edible food and sea urchins.

Continuity and the notions of deities, gods and God represent profound leaps in the evolution of human culture. Let the histories of the world's great religious philosophies speak for themselves. Accompanied by laws that would later be engraved on stones, scrolls and in leather-bound creeds, it is a history of the human quest for a greater understanding of the creation and of its creator. Visible gods became an invisible God. Animism was replaced by theism, which in turn has been challenged by humanism and the supremacy of human rights. God moved from being outside us to being inside and then to being everywhere. Some say that He left and others that He will come back again. All things considered, the idea – or for some the conviction – of life everlasting appears to be deeply embedded in the human psyche, for, as the poet Czeslaw Milosz reminds us, "it has accompanied man in his wanderings through time. It has always been larger and deeper than religious or philosophical creeds which expressed only one of its forms."

Because of the meaning that is derived from them, the significance of the world's religions should be neither negated nor underestimated. They are far more than mere codes of conduct or moral philosophies. *Ligare*, the Latin word which means to connect or to bind and from which the word religion is derived, plays no small role in the survival of a species that knows its ultimate fate. Continuity, connection, transformation and transmutation are the hallmarks of evolution are they not? Everything in life changes its skin ... even the gods. Does it really matter that someone else's cosmology or notion of God might look a little different from yours or mine? How different that could be is reflected in these lines of a poem by Howard Nelson. The poem is called "Elephant Thoughts".

> Afterwards one of us asked
> "What is the difference between us and the elephants?"
> Many differences, as big as elephants, no doubt –
> But we sat dumb a while, not sure what to answer.
> Then one, the one who had lived with the elephants said
> "The difference is this – human beings are the only species
> that claim to be made in God's image."
> So, maybe he is an elephant. A large female
> Somewhere out on the plains
> Tossing dust onto her shoulders, surrounded by her disciples.
> Perhaps God has huge grey ears.
> Perhaps God is so massive that it seems to flow.
> Perhaps God's tusks are long, powerful, tapered arcs ...
> I've heard stranger claims.

There is at least one philosophical problem in which all thinking people are interested, wrote the historian and philosopher Bryan Magee. "It is the problem of cosmology; the problem of understanding the world – including ourselves, and our knowledge as part of the world. All science is cosmology," he said.

LOOKING BACK

The dinosaurs might be gone but they are not forgotten for the Earth, it would seem, does not forget her children. Their signatures, along with those of our mammalian predecessors, are not only written in our genes but they can also be found in the anatomy and chemistry of the human brain. Their imprint, as we shall see, is still wet and very much with us.

In the 1960s, in a fascinating yet sobering analysis of the evolution of the brain, Paul Maclean introduced the notion of the human brain as an organ that has retained its reptilian and paleo-mammalian origins. The human brain, he said, is a Triune Brain. In other words, the human animal, to this day, operates with three "brains" – a reptilian brain, an early mammalian one and a neo-mammalian, or human, one. According to Maclean, each of these brains has its own memory, motor functions, intelligence and its own sense of time and space. The boundaries between the three levels of brain functioning

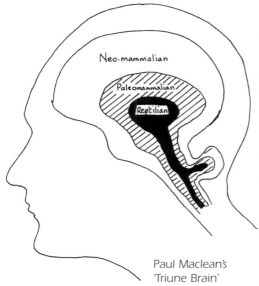

Paul Maclean's 'Triune Brain'

are obviously not as rigid as the diagram portrays but in the light of an ecological intelligence, the concept is both useful and important.

The reptilian brain of crocodiles, lizards and snakes, including the extinct dinosaurs, has changed little in its 180 to 220 million-year history. Its anatomy consists chiefly of a brainstem and other nuclei responsible for the rhythm of the heart, breathing, co-ordinating fight and flight responses and for the interpretation of perceptual stimuli such as sounds, movement and particularly that of olfaction – the ancient sense of smell. Although our sense of smell compared with our other senses appears to have lost the survival significance that it still holds for our reptilian and mammalian cousins (elephants can smell water more than thirty kilometres away), these other reptilian nuclei remain intact and functional in the brains of the human animal. And yet our sense of smell, in spite of its lack of potency, is nevertheless an important one. Odours and fragrances of all sorts, from wax crayons, pencil shavings, peanut butter sandwiches, egg and bacon, body scents and perfumes to the smell of the first rains are powerful reminders of one's culture, one's community and even one's identity.

As we compare the evolution and behaviour of the living creatures on our planet, it is important that we remember that the game we are playing is a shared one. It is called *survival*. In this light, when we snootily describe the behaviour of reptiles and other creatures as being instinctive with a tendency to be automatic, we would do well to acknowledge our own brainstem behaviour. Yes, it is likely that crocodiles are unemotional, but we too are capable of cold-blooded indifference. Yes, reptiles do tend to be opportunistic with little or no cognitive appreciation of the present, the future or of past events, but we too have an eye for the gap. "I want it all, and I want it now" is the brainstem speaking. We too are territorially and materially acquisitive, often getting what we want by acts of intimidation and threat displays, otherwise known as bullying and blackmail.

Yes, reptiles are naturally prejudiced in favour of brainstem drives, but they are anything but unintelligent. Take the modern Nile crocodile of tropical Africa, Asia and Australia, *Crocodylus niloticus*, for example. It has been on Earth at least fifty times longer than us, outliving countless species that have come and gone during their remarkable tenure. These creatures can remain under water for up to forty-five minutes and with their short, mobile ear-flaps acting like volume controls, their hearing is better than any other reptile. They continue to grow throughout their lives and an adult crocodile, by utilising the accumulated fat in its long tail, is capable of going without food for up to two years. What is more, it can determine the sex of its oviparous (egg-born) offspring according to the depth at which the female lays her eggs in the sand. Males are born from the shallower and therefore warmer levels of the conical-shaped hole in which the crocodile lays her eggs, females from the deeper levels. What kind of intelligence accounts for these extraordinary capacities? There is a "crocodile" in me and it shows itself in my drives, my impulsiveness, my compulsions, my deceptiveness and my guile. Consciousness and intelligence, as we shall see, are not to be confused.

Although the Earth's earliest known mammals such as the mouse-like climber, *Eomaia scansoria*, made their appearance about seven cosmic months ago (125 million years), it was the onset of the Tertiary epoch, sixty-five million years ago, that coincided with the rapid emergence of what Maclean calls the "second brain" – the convoluting brain of the warm-blooded Class Mammalia. Called the paleo-mammalian brain, this new and larger structure gave its owners a more sophisticated range of motor functions, emotions, memory and a sense of place, but everything "id" – everything impulsive – about its reptilian origins, came along with it. The main characteristic of this new brain was a consolidation of the widespread connections between the autonomic centres for body homeostasis such as hunger/satiety, sleep/wakefulness etc and those of smell, sight and taste. But there was more. The other anatomical changes included a fairly well defined positioning of the hypothalamus – the hormone-primed seat of the emotions associated with aggression, flight, anticipation, passivity and caregiving. It also included the significant consolidation of the links between those delicate neurological structures and chemicals associated with learning and the retention of memory. This new brain became associated with important changes in animal socialisation. It became part and parcel not only of the socially significant differentiation of audio-vocal calls into those of alarm, contact, comfort, separation and sexual communication, but to an increase in the sophistication of co-operative care for the young as well. On top of that, this new brain heralded what is arguably the most outstanding behavioural difference between reptiles and mammals – the capacity for play.

A long a spectrum of rough and tumble games, ambushing, chasing and hide-and-seek, every mammal in its own way knows how to play. Play has its neurological substrate in the thalamic region of the limbic system and its contribution towards the survival of each mammalian species is a profound one. Looked at a little more critically, play is about affiliation and bonding, about prowess, future ranking and the honing of skills. It is also a mode of self-discovery, of finding one's physical boundaries and limitations, of games that end up with tears and of establishing rules – ask any child who grew up with brothers and sisters. Play and learning go hand in hand. Through play we stretch not only our muscles but, through word play, our vocabulary and our imagination as well. And lest we forget, word play is central to political and economic one-upmanship. Let no one say there is no point in play ...

> The wilderness says
> "Don't fool yourself!"
> To play
> is an ancient dress rehearsal
> for the kill.

Like the brain of their reptilian relatives, the paleo-mammalian brain, too, is not concerned with the poetry of moonlight. It is not concerned with meaning or the philosophical significance of events, but it nevertheless carries the early chemistry of fair play. One only has to spend time with wolves, elephants, baboons and chimpanzees to recognise in their social systems that these animals, especially the females, are aware of the difference between acceptable and unacceptable behaviour within their groups. In other words, it would appear that somewhere in the transition between the second and the third brain, justice and morality – a sense of right and wrong – begins to define itself.

To illustrate this, Sarah Brosnan, a doctoral research worker at the Yerkes National Primate Centre in Atlanta, Georgia, has come up with some fascinating evidence to support the evolutionary significance of fair play. Working with South American capuchin monkeys, *Cebus apella*, she devised an experiment where pairs of female capuchins were trained to exchange stones for pieces of cucumber. This in itself was significant, for as Brosnan reminds us, not many species are willing to relinquish their possessions intentionally. She then changed the experiment. Dividing the monkeys into two groups, she placed them in separate but adjacent cages. The reason for this was that the capuchins in one group would be able to observe the exchanges between the handler and their colleagues in the other group. Brosnan then deliberately changed the stones-for-food formula in one of the groups. In exchange for their stones, she began rewarding group A with grapes while continuing to reward group B with cucumber. Her bias went even further when, in some instances, she purposely rewarded the "favoured" group for not having performed at all. The cucumber group meanwhile, hoping to earn a higher salary (grapes) in exchange for their products (stones) continued to get paid in cucumbers. Unfair? The monkeys certainly thought so. What follows is amazing but not surprising. The cucumber group stopped their exchanges with the handler, preferring to withhold their stones rather than be given an inferior reward. As the experiment progressed, not only did Group B refuse the cucumber, in some cases they hurled the unwanted food at the handler. In this patently biased experiment, it is not difficult to imagine human beings responding in the same way. It tells us a lot about the evolutionary origins of trade unions and revolution.

We come now to the emergence of the neo-mammalian brain – that incredible matrix beneath our skulls without which there would be no sense of music, mercy, morality or meaning. What is it that makes us different to our animal brothers and sisters and where should we look to find the answer? I suggest we look once more at the human genome and to our nearest primate cousin, the chimpanzee, *Pan troglodytes*. If the genetic difference between a human and a chimpanzee is as little as two percent, then that tiny fraction has to be seen as colossal. We might as well be comparing different galaxies, for within that fractional difference lies a consciousness that is uniquely human. We are indeed creatures of the wild, but unlike our animal kin – and thanks to those additional convolutions of grey matter, especially the frontal lobe (the chimpanzee has vastly less of it) – we have become creatures of culture and conscience also. Remove the convoluted frontal cortex from a human brain and you will be faced with an individual who is both disturbed and disturbing, grossly lacking in insight and without any sense of consequence. Without the frontal lobe, we lose what is arguably the most important ability of human socialisation – the capacity to deliberately inhibit or to delay our actions. Take away the frontal lobe and we lose our ability to say, "Wait a minute ... let's think about it". We lose our ability to regulate our behaviour.

But what is consciousness? This is an ancient question and because it is a subject that is both philosophical and physiological, any definition is going to be contentious. For a start, most of our perceptions, interpretations and responses to the world around us are in fact unconscious – we are not aware that we are doing them. Does this mean that these activities are not a part of consciousness? The answer, of course, is no. Consciousness, if understood as evolutionary and survival-oriented, must obviously include these hugely important "unconscious" attributes. It should also be obvious that certain aspects of consciousness are shared by all mammals.

We will deal with the subject of the "unconscious" in the following chapter, but because it could help to tease out the difference between human consciousness and that of other animals, I invite the reader to see consciousness in its awakened state. In other words, without demeaning the role of the unconscious, I wish to equate our varying levels of consciousness with varying levels of *awareness*. In a hierarchy, to be conscious includes being awake (level one), being alert (second level), aware (third level), self-aware (fourth) and finally, aware that we are aware (level five). It is obvious that to be alive and effective, every living creature needs to be functional in at least the first three levels, and for "higher" animals, including humans, the first four. Mediated through the senses of sight, smell, touch, taste and hearing, the first three levels are essential for a consciousness of external stimuli and events – the movement of an impala, the alarm call of a francolin, the smell of meat, of oestrus and the taste of blood. The fourth level, to be self-aware, implies an awareness, however crude or rudimentary, of one's *internal* state. It is to be aware of the emotion or feeling-charged chemistry of hunger, thirst, sleep, sexual desire, protection and escape and of being able to link this awareness to the external environment. It is important to remember that the awareness of one's external environment is associated with emotion-charged nuclei in the evolutionary oldest part of our brains, the brainstem – a reminder that any creature with a brainstem has feelings.

The next level of awareness – to be aware that you are aware – is a massive jump from the fourth level. Dependent on the other levels of awareness, it describes a consciousness that can reflect upon itself, upon its history, its nature and its co-existence with other creatures. Think about yourself for a moment. How do you see yourself, or expect to see yourself when you look into a mirror? Is that you looking back and what is that smudge of paint doing on your cheek? If you lean forward toward the mirror and watch yourself removing the smudge, then you are not only self-aware, but aware that you are aware. You understand the concept of "me". That is "me" in the mirror. Surely such a consciousness sets us apart from our primate cousins? Well, the answer is no. Chimpanzees recognise their own reflections. It either knows, or soon learns upon looking into a mirror, that a blob of paint, deliberately daubed onto its forehead, belongs to it. It will also, in the same way that we groom ourselves, observe itself removing the blob until the image in the mirror is to its satisfaction. All other animals, on the other hand, with the possible exception of the African elephant and other primates like gorillas, seem to be utterly indifferent to their reflections. Instead, their consciousness is geared to the level of being awake, alert and aware of what is going on outside the notion of a personal identity. This should not be construed as believing that animals are not aware of an internal world of feelings or that they are unintelligent. They do have feelings and they are intelligent. Aware of the frustration that comes with the failure to get what it wants, most animals are quite capable of engaging in problem solving as well as attending to certain stimuli rather than others. For example, wolves, dogs, elephants and primates are known to initiate and terminate behavioural and cognitive activities such as play and herding, as well as assisting an injured or handicapped companion, including human companions. In his book, *Good Natured*, Frans de Waal describes a chimpanzee offering guidance to a blindfolded handler by leading the handler by the hand to a source of food. Few will doubt that this kind of action is an example of fairly sophisticated thought processing or, if you like, a higher consciousness.

So, what really separates us from other animals? Let's go back to that mirror. The difference between humans and our animal kin is probably related to the way that we look at ourselves in a mirror. It relates to the questions we ask of ourselves and to the stirring of the imagination when we peer into that looking glass. For instance, "*How* did that blob of paint get there? *Who* put it there, and *why*? And what about the face that looks back? When studying your reflection, do you recognise someone who had a little bit too much to drink at last night's party, or wonder what happened to the youthful features that used to look back at you? Do you promise yourself that you are going to spend more time with the family or that you need a holiday?

With that objective image of "me" looking back, an entirely subjective world comes into play and the result is a kind of dialogue or interaction with oneself. And it is ongoing. The world, in effect, becomes a mirror.

With the realisation that we are constantly interacting with the world, we are able to put ourselves into it, to see our reflections in it and to reflect upon them. But we are also interested in what is going on behind the mirror. From astrology to the reading of tea leaves, we are constantly trying to decode and recode what we perceive to be the intentions of Nature. I don't know that there is any other animal that is quite so analytical and speculative. Yes, other animals too, have memories and some of them have dreams, but can they reflect upon their mortality? Can they speculate about their future? Can they say, "Hey, I wonder where I'll be this time tomorrow?" To be aware that you are aware, or, to be more precise, to be aware that you are aware that I am aware of what you are aware of etc, is the neurological legacy of an ancestor that began to understand the deeper significance of relationships and of time – yesterday, today and tomorrow – and with that, the need to consciously plan for tomorrow. It was the gift of sequential thinking and of the moulding of words into past, present and future tenses. It marked the beginning of experimental science, of music and stories that begin "Once upon a time..." It was the beginning of an understanding of the impermanence of life, of cosmologies, philosophies, of the human need for continuity and of what would become organised religions. It was the redefining of the human identity. Without sequential thought and language, our ability to create ideas, symbols and concepts about our world would not only be severely impaired, but in all likelihood, impossible. Without language, it is unlikely that we could maintain an identity that is personal. To me, that fifth level of consciousness and language go hand in hand.

What else can we find in that genetic fraction between us and our troglodyte cousins that might qualify us for a consciousness that is different to the rest of the animal kingdom? Perhaps the following attributes are the ones that make it so: aware that we are never far from the edge of the unknown, that we are mortal, and that we are not the masters of our fate, we are the only creatures that create humour out of our fate. As far as we know, we are the only species that contemplates an afterlife.

We also appear to be the only animals capable of imagining what we might become, of seeing beyond ourselves and, as if pulled by that vision, of daring to go for it. We are the only animals I know where food, water and air will never be enough for an existence that is meaningful and who have therefore learned to feed off their imagination and their dreams.

Looking back upon our molecular origins, to our geology, to those first cellular membranes and to the eventual expression of a species capable of reflecting upon itself, it would appear that we are indeed the "salt of the Earth", as St Matthew put it, not just in soul, but in science also. The relationship of the principal cations (the electropositive elements) in the blood serum of all animals, as well as of man, is constant. It is calcium : sodium : potassium = 5 : 10 : 160. This is a close representation of their respective proportions in seawater, differing only by a greater content of magnesium in the oceans as we know them today. According to McCallum's theory in 1901 (no known relation to the author) this difference can be explained by the low precipitations of ocean magnesium in the Cambrian epoch just prior to the emergence of organisms from the surrounding water onto the land 550 to 570 million years ago.

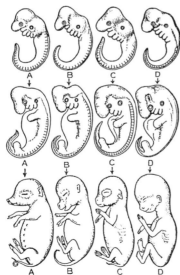

Four mammalian embryos at various stages of development: A, hog; B, calf; C, rabbit; D, human. (Villee: from Romanes' "Darwin and After Darwin," after Haeckel, with the permission of the Open Court Publishing Company.)

The animals, then, are in us and with us; we share their genes and their juices. Made up of countless molecules, cells and complex organs, each one of us is the carrier not only of the pattern of embryonic gill slits and tails, but the entire history of life also. It would appear that the aboriginal "water of life" still circulates in the blood of every animal, including us. To me it is both exciting and humbling to acknowledge that the sophisticated cells, tissues, organs and systems of the living creatures of our time have their origins in the single-cell organisms that adapted to life on Earth nearly three billion years ago. It should not be that difficult to imagine, either. After all, suggests Lynn Margulis, "the fertilised human cell begins as a single water-borne cell which then begins to divide, taking only forty weeks to differentiate into a creature that is capable of living in air". It would appear that we are, indeed, cosmic mongrels, a little bit of this ... a little bit of that. I agree with the writer and philosopher Jorge Luis Borge who wrote: "We would do well to practice a sublime astronomy ... for if we see the Milky Way it is because it actually exists in our souls."

And so, where were you when the foundations of the Earth were being laid? Linked to the molecular and chemical origins of this planet, one way of answering this question is to reply that, in essence, we were all there and we are still there. Every hydrogen atom in our bodies originates from the time of the Big Bang; every atom of iron in our red blood cells is a leftover of supernova explosions; every atom of oxygen and carbon is a gift from our sun. Psychologically, those foundations are being laid right now. They are the foundations of a new way of thinking about who and what we are in relationship to the Earth and to Nature. And we are the masons of the way we think. We can say yes and no.

You ask what time it is – it is time to pray

Rumi

3

THE WAKE-UP CALLS

F EW WILL ARGUE THAT THIS PAST MILLENNIUM HAS BEEN WITNESS TO SOME of the most dramatic changes to the way human beings have come to see themselves in their relationship to the world. The catalyst in this process has been the questioning or reflective nature of human consciousness itself, but more especially the thinking of certain rare and courageous individuals to whom we are greatly indebted. They are responsible for what I believe to be the five major wake-up calls of the past five hundred years (one cosmic minute).

The first wake up call, triggered by the Polish astronomer, Nicolaus Copernicus (1473–1543) promulgated the now accepted theory that the Earth and the planets rotate around the sun – not the other way round. In short, he was announcing the news that the Earth had lost its fancied position as the centre of the universe. This must have caused great philosophical discomfort to many, particularly the church, who saw the Earth and humans as central to God's universe. Years later, in an astonishing act of retribution against anyone challenging its cosmology, the church came down hard on Copernicus' successor, Galileo Galilei (1564–1642), when he excitedly announced the discovery of the moons of Jupiter. At the time the principals of the Holy Church of Rome, instead of leaping at the opportunity to peep through Galileo's telescope, refused to do so, threatening to excommunicate the embattled astronomer if he did not refute his claim. Additional death threats forced Galileo to conclude that his cause was not worth dying for, whereupon he disclaimed his new-found discovery.

Let us not judge Galileo too harshly, for we might have done the same. We are old hands at denying the truth of ourselves, of turning our heads, of refusing to turn the telescope inwards. We are all wary of the possibility of being shown up, of discovering that our perceptions have been wrong, or that our lives might have been more fulfilled if we had only been a little more daring.

Those early giants of mathematics and astronomy have been more than vindicated and we are now privy to haunting, yet magnificent, images from deep space, from time and distances that have too many noughts, too many powers of ten for our minds to assimilate. The images remind us of how small we are, how distant and how little we really know. And yet, in spite of the fact that our Earth does circle the sun and beyond that, the deep centre of our galaxy, we don't quite believe it, do we? Ironically, five hundred years on, our speech confirms that Copernicus, at a subtle level, has not been fully acknowledged. We still speak of sunrises and sunsets, unconsciously reinforcing the notion that the sun revolves around us. In the self-centred world of the human animal, we have great difficulty in speaking about the Earth rising into the night – how beautiful – or of our planet dipping sharply into the morning, saluting the sun. This is poetic speech, but it is important. It is part of the language of ecological intelligence, which is at once factual, at once poetic. To see the horizon tilting upwards and away from the sun is an entirely different experience to watching the sun going down. Try it.

The second wake up call was a little louder than the first. This was the voice of the English physicist, Isaac Newton (1642–1727), a mind that gave us the law of gravity as well as the classical laws of motion. Newton not only put the Earth in its place, but the planets, and the sun too, for they are subject to the same laws. Thanks to Newton, the universe was something that we could begin to measure – it had weight, it was gravid ... hence the word gravity, from the Latin *gravidus*, to be laden, heavy ... pregnant. For many, it was hardly a surprise that an apple would fall on one's head if one sat directly beneath it for long enough, or that a body, at rest, could be propelled by a force acting upon it. Who didn't know, or at least suspect, that for every action there was an equal and opposite reaction? On the playful side, who of us in our youth has not accelerated a reluctant playmate into a swimming pool, knowing sooner, rather than later, a more than equal and opposite reaction was on the cards?

Realizing the pregnant significance of Newton's laws, there were those who saw beyond the banality of playground physics. They knew deep down that to understand them was to have our lives changed forever. History, in this regard, has already spoken. Without Newton's signature, there might not have been space travel, aircraft, industrial engineering or technology in the way we know it today. And yet technology, for all its blessings, has come at a price – the industrial revolution and with it the growth of cities and increased urbanisation has distanced us from our relationship with the land, the rivers and the sea. This was not Newton's fault, and for everything that this man's intellect unveiled, we need to honour him. His legacy as well as that of Copernicus, has had an indelible impact on modern thought.

The third wake up call was like a thunderclap. It was the voice of the nineteenth century British naturalist, Charles Darwin (1809–1882). Compared with the largely impersonal discoveries of Copernicus, Galileo and Newton, Darwin's ideas were a lot closer to home. Most people are profoundly indifferent as to whether it is the Earth or the sun that revolves around the other and few of us would lose sleep because we didn't understand the aerodynamics of a space rocket. But it is impossible to be indifferent to Darwin. He struck a deep subjective chord and the ongoing resistance to his ideas tells us that the chord is both raw and deep.

Intrinsic to Darwin's message is the notion that evolution is something tangible, something meaningful, and that we are socially and biologically closer to our animal companions than we would like to think. The tracks along the path of the unfolding mammalian genome are undoubtedly those of Darwin. The lion is more than ninety percent human, so is the spotted hyena. The African elephant also has well over ninety per cent of the human gene sequence. But that is not all. Those pesky fruit flies of the Family Drosophila that buzz around our baskets of over-ripe fruit are forty-two percent human while the chimpanzee, our closest primate cousins, share more than ninety-eight per cent of our blueprint. Without discounting the obvious as well as the – sometimes – subtle differences in genetic expression, how much of the genome of the hyena and the chimpanzee do we have in us?

The animals, in science, as we are discovering, and in poetry as it always has been, are in our blood. The landscape is in our skin. We, too, gnash and gnaw; we sound our alarm calls and our cries of territory, sexuality and discovery. We, too, are known for our aggression, for gang-related violence, for organised warfare and, like the *Polygerus* ants in the Chirichaua Mountains in Arizona, for slavery. We, too, are defined by our territorial tiffs, known for our experience of fear, frustration and rage and by the way we are warmed by that powerful yet indescribable phenomenon called belonging – what the human animal sometimes calls soul. The sense of belonging affects creatures from antelopes to dogs, birds, elephants and primates, and we are not the only creatures who die from a loss of it.

Who spins around whom in this dance? In these selected lines from his astounding poem "Wilderness", written in 1918, the poet Carl Sandburg celebrates his animal nature – long before the unravelling of the human genome.

> There is a wolf in me ... fangs pointed for tearing gashes ... a
> red tongue for raw meat ... and the hot lapping of
> blood – I keep the wolf because the wilderness gave it
> to me and the wilderness will not let it go.
> There is a fox in me ... a silvery-gray ... fox ...I sniff and guess
> ... I pick things out of the wind and air ...
> I circle and loop and double cross.
> There is a hog in me ... a snout and a belly ... a machinery for
> eating and grunting ... a machinery for sleeping satisfied
> in the sun – I got this too from the wilderness and the
> wilderness will not let it go.

There is a fish in me ... I know I come from salt-blue-water-
gates ... I scurried with shoals of herrings ... I blew water
spouts with porpoises ... before land was ... before the
water went down ... before Noah ... before the first chapter
of Genesis
There is a baboon in me ... hairy under the arm pits
... ready to sing and give milk ... waiting – I keep the baboon
because the wilderness says so.
There is an eagle in me and a mockingbird
... and I got them from the wilderness.

O, I got a zoo, I got a menagerie, inside my ribs, under my bony
head, under my red-valve heart –
And I got something else : it is a man-child heart, a woman-
child heart: it is a father and mother
And lover: it comes from God-Knows-Where: it is going to God-
Knows-Where – for I am the
Keeper of the zoo: I say yes and no: I sing and I kill and I work:
I am a pal of the world: I come from the wilderness.

From what depths did this poem come, I wonder, if not from a deep
sensing of the bio-psychological history of the human animal? At the
level of the gene, then, more particularly in the sequencing of the
amino acids that bind the chromosomes within the gene, every living
thing speaks the same language. From flies and foxes to humans, all the
creatures of the Earth and the sea say ONE thing – we are relatives.
This, to me, is poetry. Darwin was right.

We have all had the experience of sitting bolt upright in the middle of the night, the result of a sudden yet delayed realisation of
the significance of what someone has said, written or done. It is as if,
prior to the sudden realisation, we were either resistant to or unable to
grasp what that person was trying to convey. Such was and remains the
significance of the voice and the written work of Albert Einstein

(1879–1955), a man whose double-barrelled theories of relativity represent the fourth great wake-up call of the past half-millennium.

In 1905, with the publication of his Special Theory and eleven years later, of his General Theory of Relativity, Einstein turned Newton's laws of a three-dimensional universe inside-out. With his famous special theory equation $E = mc^2$, he established that mass and energy are equivalent and that they can be transformed into each other. He also predicted that under certain circumstances time will slow down, for example as one approximates the speed of light. In this theory, he concluded that there are "hidden invariables" in the ordering of the universe. It was an admission that certain occurrences in physics could not be predicted with the solid certainty of traditional cause and effect thinking. Every measurement, he said, depends on one's frame of reference – an observation not without profound personal as well as socio-cultural significance. To a three-dimensional intelligence, this is absurd. What did this mean? In short, our common sense Newtonian view of time as an ordered sequence of moments following one upon the other, the same for everyone, had been turned on its head. Newton believed that time *anywhere, anyhow*, was a phenomenon well defined. In his own words, time was "absolute, true and mathematical, of itself and from its own nature, without relation to anything external, remains similar and immovable ..." Newton said the same about our understanding of space: "Absolute, in its own nature ... similar, and immovable..."

Nearly two hundred years after Newton, following a total eclipse of the sun on 29th May 1919, there was an excited yet humble refutation of Newton's absolutes. In one of the most famous scientific observations of this past century, the astrophysicist Sir Arthur Eddington was able, as predicted by Einstein, to show that light, as it travels close to the sun on its way from a star to the earth, is deflected by the gravitational pull of the sun. Normally, because of the sun's brilliance, we cannot see the stars in daytime, but if we could, the deflection of their light-rays, according to Einstein, would make them appear in different positions from those we would expect them to occupy. At that time, the only way to prove his theory was to measure the position of stars "close" to the sun during a total eclipse and to compare it with where they were predicted to be. Einstein was right – these stars, their light deviated by the sun, were not where they were supposed to be.

Unlike Newton, who had shown the equations that explained gravity, Einstein, when he pointed out that huge masses or forces like the sun actually warp the space and light near them, was able to show *how* gravity worked. But there was more. He showed that time would be warped also. Contrary to our experience of time as a phenomenon or dimension in its own right, independent of space and the laws of motion, Einstein linked the three dimensions of space (height, width and depth) to the dimension of time, describing it as a fourth dimension – space-time. In a four-dimensional world, he said, space, time and mass are interdependent. He put it another way :

> If you will not take the answer too seriously, and consider it only as a kind of joke, then I will explain it as follows. It was formerly believed that if all material things disappeared out of the universe, time and space would be left. According to the relativity theory, however, time and space disappear together with the things.

It is practically impossible to wrap our minds around such a notion, but Einstein had the courage to think the impossible. By predicting observable effects which, as far as we are aware, no one had ever dreamt of before, he bravely put his reputation on the line. It is crucial that we do not underestimate the boldness of his imagination, for it was truly poetic.

Time, then, is not what we think it is. According to our conventional view, only the present is real or special, but when viewed from this other, objective dimension, the past, the present and the future are equally real and present, says the theoretical physicist Paul Davis. In other words, time does not flow and not only is our notion of yesterday, today and tomorrow an illusion, but there is also no such thing as the present moment either. He points out that the arrow of time might indicate the future, but this does not imply that the arrow is moving toward the future, any more than a compass needle pointing north indicates that the compass is moving north. Instead, as difficult as it might be for us to grasp, "all of eternity is laid out in a four-dimensional block or field, composed of time and the three spatial dimensions" says Davis. This is a reminder of the "block" universe that the Greek philosopher and mathematician Parmenides had intuited nearly three thousand years earlier. Does this mean we must throw away our clocks? The answer is "no". We sense time psychologically. Yes, it is likely, under certain conditions, that time might lose its separate identity from space, but it is important to recognise that this does not mean that time is identical to the three dimensions of space, says Davis. Time and space enter into daily experience and physical theory in distinct and measurable ways. This distinction, he says, is important in the everyday world of the human animal, for it underpins the key notions of cause and effect, preventing them from being hopelessly jumbled.

At the beginning of the 1920s, writes Paul Johnson in *The History of the Modern World*, "the belief began to circulate, for the first time at a popular level, that there were no longer any absolutes: of time and space, of good and evil, of knowledge, above all of value. Mistakenly but perhaps inevitably, relativity became confused with relativism" – the notion that anything goes. No one was more distressed than Einstein by this public misapprehension. He was not a practising Jew, but he acknowledged a God, believing passionately in absolute standards of right and wrong. He also believed that Nature was teleological or purposive. "God does not play dice with the universe," was his famous quote to his friend Neils Bohr when the latter questioned him about the seeming randomness of cosmic events.

In modern science, randomness versus purpose in Nature is hotly debated. Both sides of the argument have merit. "The manifestations of life, its expressions, its forms, are so diverse that they must contain a large element of the accidental", wrote the distinguished scientist and biologist Jacob Bronowski in his book *The Ascent of Man*, "... and yet the nature of life is so uniform that it must be constrained by many necessities." Who can argue the seeming randomness of an asteroid collision with the Earth, and yet who can deny at least a hint of purpose in the ongoing cycles of life and death and the seasons of every living thing? Who knows, Nature might indeed have a purpose, but it is certainly not in accordance with what the human animal would like it to be.

If Nature does have a purpose then we have to accept that we are a part of it. If not, then it is likely that we will give it one. It is part of the psychological integrity and survival of our peculiar species. For example, why is it that whenever there is a call to assist in the preservation and conservation of an endangered species, men and women rally to this call? If it is the purpose of Nature for animals to go extinct, then why not let the animals go extinct? Why not let the wilderness vanish? Because there is something in the human psyche that says no. It would seem that there is something in us that acknowledges the purpose of a whale, an elephant or a butterfly. But what purpose? At a lecture at the University of Cape Town in 1982, the author Laurens van der Post answered this question pointedly. Referring to the psychological integrity of the human being, he said, "The conservation of animals and plants is more important to human beings than we are to them. These forms of life are vital for our survival."

Roderick Frazer Nash, a former professor of History and Environmental Studies at the University of California, Santa Barbara, framed it differently during a lecture on the philosophy of wilderness in 1987. He invited listeners to think about the values of wilderness (which in the same lecture he had previously outlined factually) in terms of an analogy with a woman who asks, "Why do you love me?"

> ... try telling her that you worship her, that you cherish the life you have lived together, that she is necessary for your mental welfare, that her presence in your life makes you different, that in her own special way she is beautiful, that

she inspires you to be creative, and that she challenges you and offers you an alternative to the way most other women are in the world.

Pushing the envelope of human consciousness does not come without a price and neither did the formula $E = mc^2$. That same equation, filled with mathematical and poetic insight, was pregnant with a mushroom-shaped shadow that was to become the blueprint for the atomic bomb and nuclear war – grave and gravid stuff. It is no wonder that Einstein, at the end of his life, said that there were times when he wished he had been a simple watchmaker. However, in support of a great man, let us look again at that equation.

$E = mc^2$ was in fact a multiple pregnancy, incubating the exciting field of quantum theory, a system of mechanics based on the wave-particle duality of matter and radiation. The duality phenomenon is also known as the observer effect. In other words, light can be seen to travel in waves or particles, depending on the intention of the observer. The theory introduces us to the concept of an invisible "field" to explain the astonishing, non-classical behaviour of sub-atomic particles. As if connected or supported in a "field" of interaction, the behaviour of these particles is such that there seems to be no usual cause and effect relationship between them. In other words, their influence, one upon the other, is instantaneous. Absurd? Read on ...

Another characteristic of the behaviour of sub-atomic particles is that they manifest in quantum leaps. This is another way of saying that there is no apparent movement of the particle from point A to point B. In what could be a hint of what the poets refer to as a web of life, a particle therefore manifests or unveils itself at point B as if it had always been there. Then there is the observer effect, a phenomenon reminding us that the very act of observing particles causes them to manifest. The act of observation creates the space-time event, telling us that every sub-atomic particle exists firstly in a virtual state, the actual state manifesting itself in accordance with the intention of the observer.

Standing on the shoulders of Einstein, the German physicist Werner Heisenberg proposed his Uncertainty Principle, a theory informing us that we can know the motion or velocity of an electron and we can know its position, but we cannot know both at the same time. This principle predicts that the harder one tries to scrutinize the movements of a subatomic particle, the more elusive it becomes. The mere act of focussing on the particle is enough to disturb it. This conclusion was based on the understanding that waves of light could not be emitted at an arbitrary rate but only in "packets" called quanta, and that each quantum had a certain amount of energy that was greater the higher the frequency of the waves.

Stephen Hawking provides one of the most accessible explanations of the uncertainty principle in his classic, *A Brief History of Time*.

> In order to predict the future position and velocity of a particle, one has to be able to measure its present position and velocity accurately. The obvious way to do this is to shine light on the particle. Some of the waves of light will be scattered by the particle and this will indicate its position. However, one will not be able to determine the position of the particle more accurately than the distances between the wave crests of light, so one needs to use light of a short wavelength in order to measure the position of the particle precisely ...[but] one cannot use an arbitrarily small amount of light; one has to use a quantum. This quantum will disturb the particle and change its velocity in a way that cannot be predicted. Moreover, the more accurately one measures the position, the shorter the wavelength of light that one needs and hence the higher the energy of a single quantum. So the velocity of the particle will be disturbed by a larger amount. In other words, the more accurately you try to measure the position of the particle, the less accurately you can measure its speed, and vice versa ... Heisenberg's Uncertainty Principle is a fundamental, inescapable property of the world.

Ultimately it is impossible to know exactly how the constituents of matter are behaving. "As soon as I say: IT IS REAL, it vanishes", said Octavio Paz when asked to define the essence of poetry. And then there is the Columbian writer Gabriel Garcia Marquez, who raised a glass of wine to toast his wife: "I know you so well," he said, "that I haven't a clue who you are." The physicist and the poet ... I wonder which is which ... who spins around whom? Such is the language of poetry and of physics.

The "hidden invariables" of relativity and quantum theory preceded the "hidden order" of what is known in physics today as Chaos Theory, a fascinating discovery of the nature of turbulence, irregularity and randomness in our lives. Invariably defined as an absence of order, we do not sit easily with the notion of chaos. However, it now appears that chaos, when looked at differently, can be seen to have its own dynamic, its own order, and that there are special patterns of regularity in what we perceive as being irregular or random. It would appear that strange laws of chaos exist behind most of the things we consider remarkable about our world – the human heartbeat, human thought, storms, the structures of galaxies, the creation of a poem, cloud build-up, traffic congestion, the impact of elephants on woodlands, the rise and fall of wild dog populations, the spread of a forest fire, a winding coastline, and even the origins and evolution of life itself.

Depending on the intensity of one's focus, what might appear as an orderly situation at one level of magnification is turbulent, irregular or chaotic at another. Psychologically, any prolonged focus on any one thing, be it a person, a fantasy or a situation, is a good definition of a neurosis, a reminder that we have to learn how to vary the focus if we are to see the bigger picture in our situations. "Do no thing in excess," says Apollo. Vary your focus every now and then. Do some scanning for a change.

Chaos theory says yes and no. It reminds us that whatever interpretation we make about our perceptions of the world we can be sure that there is information missing. It tells us that the truths we seek can never be fully grasped. It reminds us also of the transformational significance of the missing information, of the dormant treasures within it – when we are open to it. It is clear to me that the pre-Christian era Greek writer Xenophanes, in this two thousand-year-old untitled poem translated by Karl Popper, understood the significance of missing information and of uncertainty ...

> The gods did not reveal, from the beginning,
> All things to us, but in the course of time
> Through seeking we may learn and know things better.
> But as for certain truth, no man has known it,
> Nor shall he know it, neither of the gods
> Nor yet of all the things of which I speak.
> For if by chance he were to utter
> The final truth, he would himself not know it...

Because quantum theory appeals to that which is deeply intuitive in us, Einstein initiated a revolution that would challenge the way we think about ourselves and about our world. It was an invitation to think differently about space, time and uncertainty. And yet most of us find this extremely difficult. Why? Because it is inconvenient, because we've got used to living in an ego-oriented, three-dimensional world where the past is behind us, to be forgotten, and where the future is out of our hands. For many, the only time that interests us is now. The only space of concern is the one we occupy. Usually, it doesn't matter what happens in the rest of the world or to the environment, unless or until it affects us directly. Sadly, this attitude has been central to the perpetuating causes of our current environmental crises. It is nothing short of what can be described as a lethal environmental lethargy. It is easy to plead ignorance with regard to what we are doing to the land, the sky and the seas, but it does not make us innocent. Ignorance is not bliss. Ignorance has been the catalyst in practically every environmental mishap of this past century.

It is time to take Nature seriously – to develop a sensitivity not only to our macrocosmic world of cause and effect but to other realities also, to the world of the small, where uncertainty and the observer effect is taken personally. It is time to stop squirming away from the uncomfortable realisation that we live in two worlds: a three-dimensional world of measured meaning and another, a curving, four-dimensional world of uncertainty. Absurd? The answer is "no". It is no more absurd than the proven theory that light possesses both the qualities of waves and particles and that it can be any one of two things at the same time.

The thorns of the ziziphus remind us that we live a dual existence. The DNA molecule itself, the essence of biological life, comes as a double helix. Ours is a world of process, of paradox, a dual world of macro and micro space, of signs and symbols, of clockwork reality and of another, equally important, reality, where time and causality have a different meaning. If we are genuine about rediscovering ourselves in Nature, then there is only one thing to do. We have to commit ourselves to the process. We have to hold the tension that comes with a dual existence, no matter what. If this sounds true, then "Say yes quickly!" urges the poet Rumi "...Inside you there's an artist you don't know about."

Inside you there's an artist you don't know about? If this rings true then it is likely that you are interested in that other vast field of uncertainty – depth psychology.

Enter Sigmund Freud (1856–1939) and Carl Jung (1875–1961), two courageous twentieth-century pioneers of depth psychology, both of them drawn to clinical medicine and healing, both of them turning the "telescope" inwards in their attempts to comprehend the dynamics of human nature. Between them, what they saw and how they articulated it serves as the fifth great wake-up call of the past six hundred years. It was a dual contribution, one from a mentor and the other from a disciple who would inevitably go his own way. Between them, they tried to make sense of another space, another great wilderness – the human psyche.

Freud, who coined the term psychoanalysis, gave us the words ego, superego and id to describe his tripartite division of the human personality. The id, a word and suffix first used by the German biologist G Weismann in 1893 to describe a unit of germ plasm, was borrowed by Freud to describe the uncultured, instinctual impulses of human behaviour. He was referring to our brainstem oriented animal nature. He described the ego as that part of the human psyche that corresponds most closely to one's autobiographical self – a controlling self that holds back the impulsiveness of the id in an effort to delay gratification until it can be found or expressed in socially approved ways. This was another way of describing the "dialogue", or tension, between the inhibitory frontal lobe and the brainstem demands for immediate gratification. The superego, he said, was that part of the personality that corresponds to the notion of conscience, the part that controls and censors one's behaviour through learned moral and social values. The pull of the superego is much more towards one's culture and conventional wisdom than to one's biology. Freud was well aware of this, for he recognized in this tension, the seeds of human neuroses. He proposed that the neuroses of civilized men and women resulted from the alienation of our egos (including the superego) from our primal, animal drives. In other words, we ignore our biological origins at great cost to our mental health. He was describing the consequences of the Human-Nature split.

In his analysis of human behaviour, however, Freud went deeper than the ego. Putting his credibility at stake, he became the recognized spokesperson for that potentially fathomable realm of the human psyche – the unconscious. He saw it as the home of hidden agendas, the domain of repressed personal memories, motivations and wishes, the reservoir from which our dreams and fantasies originate, as well as the source of what came to be known as "Freudian slips". These are those memorable words or intentions that we deliberately try to suppress but which, in certain social settings, we inexplicably and embarrassingly let slip or act out.

In support of what he believed was the universality of the role of the unconscious mind in human behaviour, Freud turned to mythology. His famous analysis of Sophocles' *Oedipus Rex* led the way to a plausible yet controversial theory of human psycho-sexual development. Drawing on an aspect of the famous Greek myth where the hero unwittingly murders his father and marries his mother, he coined the now famous "Oedipus complex" to describe the unconscious sexual attachment of infants to parents of the opposite sex. He dared to propose that all infants relive the theme of this ancient myth in that they subconsciously wish for the murder or death of the parent/competitor of the same sex in order to have the other all to themselves. It is easy, steeped as we are in the taboos of society, more especially the incest taboo (the title of one of Freud's books), to dismiss his incestuous/murderous theory as distasteful and nonsensical. However, when we care to think about it, it is not that far-fetched. It is only in rare exceptions that children do not want their mothers – their breasts, their approval, their security and so on – all to themselves. It is at the root of sibling rivalry and of the way that children can, for their own benefit, play one parent off against the other. It is primal behaviour which, properly parented, is nothing to be ashamed of.

While Freud and Jung, as we shall see, differed in their interpretation of the depths and the function of the unconscious, both men understood dreams to be the language of this mostly hidden domain. Both of them treated our strange nocturnal images seriously, believing that they were invaluable as pointers to the uncovering of repressed memories, wishes and conflicts when assessing the mental status of their patients. For both men, to *know thyself* was impossible without an understanding of one's dreams.

In his description of the causes of human neuroses, Freud sometimes came across as pessimistic, a genius embroiled with theories of death wishes, of deep-seated envy and anger in young males with regard to their fathers and of unexpressed sexual frustration in women. However, to put this into perspective, we need to remember the period in which he was living. It was called, ironically, the Victorian era, a patriarchal period of intense suppression of the feminine, a time when women were disenfranchised, when "decent" ladies covered themselves from chin to foot, and when feminine protest was dismissed as "hysterical", from the Greeg *hysterikos* – the wandering womb. A brave, brilliant and lonely man, Freud pushed the envelope of self-awareness in a way that no one before him had dared to do. As with Darwin, it is impossible to be indifferent to Freud and although his theories remain contentious, his influence in modern psychology is indelible.

Carl Jung introduced the collective unconscious, archetypes, projections, individuation and the concept of the human "shadow" into our psychological vocabulary. Like Freud, Jung was and remains contentious and for similar reasons. Pioneers of the science of subjectivity, unafraid to examine the dark side of human nature, what they had to say about the human psyche was very new and it wasn't particularly pleasant. They both had a huge respect for the symbolic as well as the emotional world of humans. But they also differed.

If Freud was revolutionary, Jung was evolutionary, and it is in this light that I believe the full significance of the latter's contribution to modern thinking is yet to be acknowledged. Extending Freud's notion of the individual psyche comprising the ego and an unconscious domain that was strictly personal, i.e. a reservoir of repressed personal memories, Jung suggested that the unconscious mind, in addition to the personal unconscious, included a vast "collective" dimension as well. He called it the collective unconscious. It was a tacit acknowledgement of the evolution of consciousness, more especially the more-than-two-million-year psychological history of our species. Irrespective of creed or culture, he believed the collective unconscious to be the domain of survival-oriented memories, myths, motifs and patterns of behaviour common to all humans. Jung called these ancient survival patterns the archetypes. To understand the significance of these survival patterns is to have a better understanding of human nature. It is to understand why human myths, fairy tales and legends are so important to us. It is to have a better understanding of the forces behind vocation and the human search for meaning.

From the Greek *archetypos*, first-moulded/original, the archetypes are the psychological equivalents of our biological drives or instincts. Genetically primed, they are a product of the collective history of human existence, of language, memories and the human ability to adapt. Jung recognized them in our uniquely varying but patterned responses to situations of conflict, danger, distress, nurturance, disorder, need, falling in love, competition and so on. Always emotionally charged, I see them linked to at least seven well-established basic emotional "command systems" in the limbic part of our brains. Elegantly described by the neurobiologist Jaak Panskepp, these systems are survival-oriented, interdependent, complementary, compensatory, and they exist in every mammal. The situations that trigger them are therefore archetypal. Panskepp divided these into systems of:

- Seeking, involving the emotions associated with curiosity, interest, expectations and the possibility of reward;
- Pleasure-lust and the associated emotions activated by achieving what has been sought;
- Anger-rage and the range of emotions triggered by the frustration of failed gratification;
- Fear-anxiety and the emotions associated with having to deal with the frustration;
- Panic-distress and the range of emotions associated with loss, sorrow, separation;
- Care and the emotions surrounding protection and nurturance;
- Play and the emotions associated with rough-and-tumble, competition and learning;

Panskepp's work is a reminder that the survival role of feelings and emotions in humans and other animals should not be underplayed or ignored for, as the neuropsychologists Mark Solms and Oliver Turnbull write, we not only *experience* emotions, we *express* them. Our emotionally-charged perceptions make us want to "do something". And we do so in many ways – fighting, fleeing, hiding, laughing, challenging, crying, blushing etc. They add: "The perceptual aspect of emotion has a compulsive effect on us. We simply cannot lie back and feel our emotions." Gripped by the impulse to respond, the historical archetypal pattern, be it of a hero, mother, father, saviour, lover – as many archetypes as there are situations – is activated in the psyche of the doer. The spontaneous act of "doing something" is an archetypal act. From altruism to opportunism, they are re-enactments of ancient motifs, themes and patterns that are evolutionary and of profound survival significance. They cannot be called upon at will. Instead, because they arise from the *felt* experience of lived events in actual lives, they constellate spontaneously as the psychic expressions of instinctual processes. The archetypes give our biological drives a human face.

To honour the gods, then, is also to honour the archetypes. But that is our choice. We are not automatons. Learning is an important part of our survival as well and, as we know, in the process of becoming more aware of our emotional responses, it becomes less difficult to predict the situations in which they will be aroused. This means as we feel ourselves being drawn into a situation we can choose to modify our response. We can learn to say yes and no to the archetypes.

And so, what does the depth psychology of Freud and Jung, more especially Jung's notion of a collective unconscious and the archetypes, have to do with ecological intelligence? Firstly, it is a reminder that the human psyche is a part of the evolutionary process. Secondly, it adds insight to the importance of psychological thinking – of developing a greater awareness of how and why we think and behave as we do and, more importantly, of allowing ourselves to be changed by that awareness. Thirdly, it introduces the notion of a collective consiousness and the implication that we exist in a "field" of information and influence, what I call a mindfield. Finally, if we are to take the admonition "know thyself" to heart, it will help us to understand a little better two crucial archetypes of Jung's analytical psychology – the Self and the shadow.

Jung described the Self with a capital 'S'. He recognized it as a phenomenon historically older than the ego and out of which the ego evolved or developed. The Self is an archetype representing not only integration or movement towards wholeness and towards a personality that is unique, but also the organizing, survival force of Nature in every individual. To me, this, more than the ego-self, is the Self that Apollo in his admonition was urging us to know.

To know this Self is a life-long process – what Jung called the process of "individuation". Marie-Louise Von Franz, an analyst and long-time colleague of Jung, described this process as "… discovering what it means to be authentic, of discovering that which can only be given by the Self – one's vocation and with it, one's natural authority". In this light individuation also implies, in every individual, the possibility of an emerging ecological intelligence. Individuation means coming to know, little by little, that we are not the masters of our fate, but we can choose our attitude towards it. Dylan Thomas, for example, made his attitude clear in the famous lines of his poem:

> Do not go gentle into that good night …
> Rage, rage against the dying of the light.

And then there is the Greek writer and poet, Kazantzakis:

> I am but a bow in your hand, Lord.
> Do not leave me
> For I will rot.
> Do not bend me beyond my strength
> For I will break
> But bend me beyond my endurance
> And let me break.

Individuation is ultimately a humbling process. As it is with insight, so it is with individuation – it is unlikely that we ever fully achieve it. It is as if, from time to time, we can touch it but we can never quite grasp it. In other words, we never become "individuated". It is therefore not about perfection or about putting an end to personal suffering. Instead, it is a process of learning to see the world with "both" eyes, of waking up and of becoming conscious of the nature and the inevitability of suffering – a far better situation than to suffer blindly.

Many of our great writers and poets knew this instinctively. An example is Albert Camus' stunning analysis of the myth of Sisyphus (the man who challenged the gods and whose punishment was to push a rock up to the top of the hill only to watch it roll back down again). Camus reminds us that "to suffer one's fate consciously is to be stronger than that rock".

Individuation, then, is an individual matter but it cannot be done alone. We are, after all, a social species – we act, we interact and we abstract. It is impossible outside of humanity, outside of work and outside of relationships and that includes our relationship with the Earth and every living thing. It is ongoing. And it is difficult, for one reason more than any other – it includes the enormous task of encountering and of trying to come to terms with the human shadow – the "dark" side of our nature. To explore this side of our nature and to take it seriously is to begin a process that will inevitably lead to a profound change in the organisation of the way we think about ourselves, about social change and, by no means least, about the human-animal interface.

How many times can a man turn his head,
pretending he just doesn't see?

Bob Dylan

"The devil made me do it."

4

FACING OUR SHADOW

DESCRIBING IT AS THE SUM OF ALL THOSE UNPLEASANT QUALITIES WE like to hide from ourselves and from others, but which we readily recognise in others, Jung gave the dark side of our nature a name. Calling it our shadow, he described it as "...a moral problem that challenges the whole ego personality" and added that "...no one can become conscious of the shadow without considerable effort."

Without an understanding of the shadow effective self-examination is impossible, which is why, if we are serious about exploring the notion of an ecological intelligence, it needs to be addressed early. Who are the people and animals that *irrationally* get to you, those you instantly dislike and with whom you would rather not associate – priests, prostitutes, policemen, gargoyles, beggars, hags, hyenas, vultures or snakes? How inflated is our opinion of ourselves? How far removed from Earthiness has our self-deception taken us? These are questions that are probing for the shadow and they are important questions. Why? Because we all have something of the hag and the hyena in us. We are all, in our own subtle ways, manipulators, conmen and we all own a little bit of the beggar, too. We are pathetic, but we are also wonderful. And when we know this, when we recognise our inflation, or the scavenger, the conman and the road-rage creature within us, then we can learn how to say yes and no to them.

When we avoid entering the territory of the shadow, says the scholar and author Michael Meade, "then we begin attracting shadowy figures who will one day explode into our lives". Our shadow has deep biological roots. "At home" at the level of the brainstem, it is as if it has a life of its own. It is not interested in delayed gratification or the different shades of grey. "The shadow always wants something for nothing," says the analyst and writer Richard Chachere and, as the naturalist Lyall Watson writes in his book *Dark Nature*, "it is bound to be selfish, angry, jealous, lustful, greedy, infantile, suicidal and murderous". However, because of the energy that it generates, it is vital that we become conscious of it, that you put its energy on your side. Unacknowledged, it can be destructive. It is at the core of xenophobia and racism. Make no mistake about it, it is real. It is in our blood. We cannot escape it, for as Robert Louis Stevenson reminds us in his famous story of Dr Jekyll and Mr Hyde, wherever Jekyll goes, Hyde comes along with him. In other words, wherever the evolutionary younger forebrain goes, the older brainstem comes with it.

Stevenson's story is a shadow classic in that it tells us what happens when one's shadow is disowned. In an experiment in which Dr Jekyll concocts a potion that would separate his good side from his bad side, he discovers to his dismay that he slowly *becomes* Mr Hyde. In the end the "good" doctor takes his life, ending the life of the "bad" Mr Hyde, also.

But why do we deny or repress it in ourselves? When considering the development of the human ego, it seems that we do it because we have to. Deception, as we shall see, is part of our survival and so is self-deception. It is a subtle strategy to escape the emotions that come with self-examination and accountability and, like any strategy that is employed excessively or unconsciously, it is bound to become maladaptive.

Apart from the metaphysical association with the brainstem, it would appear that there is indeed an important neurobiological link to our psychological shadow. This link is recognizable in patients who suffer from a brain-damaged condition called the Right Hemisphere Syndrome. One of the manifestations of this syndrome is a phenomenon called anosognosia – the loss of an ability in a person to recognize that he or she has a disease or a physical defect. Sometimes paralysed down the left side of their bodies, these patients often deny that there is anything wrong with them, even to the point of delusion. Mark Solms and Oliver Turnbull, two neuropsychologists who have investigated these patients write:

If a patient who claims she is able to run is asked why she is in a wheelchair, she might respond: "There was nowhere else to sit." If asked why she is not moving her left arm, she could say something like: "I exercised it a lot today, so I'm resting it." These patients seem prepared to believe anything, so long as it excludes admitting that they are ill. Not uncommonly, they deny that their paralysed arm belongs to them, saying that it belongs to someone else. They also frequently express intense dislike and hatred toward the paralysed limb.

Sometimes, in an act reminiscent of the good Dr Jekyll trying to get rid of the bad Mr Hyde, they even go as far as to physically assault the limb. It should not be difficult to see the neurological parallels of the shadow in this example but it begs another question. Are these patients really unaware of their condition? The answer, it would seem, is "no". With one-on-one psychotherapy, what begins to emerge is that they are aware of their condition and that the denial of it stems from being unable to tolerate the emotions that arise from this awareness. Solms and Turnbull in their investigations of two of these patients write:

> In their psychotherapy sessions, both patients burst into tears for brief moments during which they seemed to be overwhelmed by emotions of the very kind that are normally conspicuous by their absence. This gave the impression of *suppressed* sadness, grief, dependency fears and so on, rather than a true *absence* of such feelings ...

The authors remind us that "you cannot come to terms with a loss if you do not acknowledge that it has happened" – an explanation that helped them in their analysis of a third patient with the same syndrome. In this instance, in the same way that we ignore or sometimes attack the targets of our negative projections, "Mrs A did have an internalised image of her damaged, crippled self, and she attacked that image to the point of twice attempting to kill herself".

To me, these examples point not only to the reality of our shadow, but to our personal fragility as well. They tragically reflect the degree to which every one of us unconsciously denies the "crippled" side of ourselves. Yes, the human ego is fragile. It needs to be defended, but at what cost to our capacity to grieve and to heal? And at what cost to the land, the animals and our fellow human beings? There may well be a survival element in the denial of our shadow, but are we really unaware of what we are doing? I don't think so. Deep down, we know that what is happening to the Earth has something to do with us.

In order that we can learn to embrace the shadow, it is important that we take a closer look at what happens when we remain unconscious of it, more especially the way in which the projection of the shadow reinforces the establishment of "out-groups", minorities and scapegoats. Unacknowledged, the shadow becomes the enemy – dangerous, disorderly, fugitive, distasteful, stupid, lacking spirituality and with no purpose beyond what is immediate. Every time we laugh at someone else's misfortune says Lyall Watson, it is our shadow showing. Every time we take pleasure in the pain of a rival, it is a genetic pleasure. Each time we display exaggerated feelings about others or behave out of character, we are seeing the genetic shadow in action. It can be frightening, even shocking, to come face to face with our dark side in these ways, but it is necessary. It is one thing to experience the pleasure of one-upmanship, it is another to get tangled up in the smugness that comes with it. It is one thing to know that we have a psychological shadow, it is another to be aware of what makes it so dangerous – *projection* – the act, albeit unintentionally, of pinning it on someone or something else.

Animal: any animal, other than man … an inhuman person; brutish or beast-like … pertaining to the physical or carnal nature of man, rather than his spiritual or intellectual nature (Hamlyn Encyclopaedic Dictionary).

One of the greatest insults to the animal kingdom is to describe unacceptable human behaviour as that of a wild animal. Hyenas and snakes, for example, are well known targets for shadow projections. In a remarkable slander of Africa's spotted hyena, *Crocus crocuta*, a recent book designed to identify corporate illness identifies a "corporate hyena" as follows:

> ... narcissistic, immature and neurotic. The corporate hyena most probably carries scars of a dysfunctional childhood [with] societal maladjustment embedded in their behaviour. The corporate hyena is a control freak ... true to the nature of scavengers and gluttons they will destroy and stuff themselves in our weaker moments.

This is anthropomorphic thinking (attributing human qualities to animals) at its worst. These are human attributes and they have nothing to do with these incredibly intelligent and social creatures. Apart from what seems to be a sad lack of knowledge about hyenas, these authors say there is nothing wrong with comparing particular types of human behaviour with that of certain animals as it is commonplace all over the world, adding that "people have come to expect colourful expressions from Africa." Indeed, comparisons are commonplace. However, there is a huge difference between comparisons and projections, which is precisely what these authors have failed to distinguish. They have projected onto hyenas the shadow qualities we are least likely to acknowledge in ourselves.

Recently, while guiding a group of international participants attending a conference at a South African game lodge, one of the delegates on a first-time visit to Africa announced that she did not want to see any hyenas or vultures. I asked her, "Why not?" and she answered, "Well ... there's something evil about them ...you can't trust them ... and hyenas are cowardly aren't they?" "Where did you get that information?" I protested. "From the movie, The Lion King," she replied, awkwardly.

I have been privileged to observe and to follow hyenas in the wild – it teaches you to see them differently. Take, for example, the interactions between lions and hyenas. On the one hand they are the ultimate competitors, both species predominantly nocturnal, both hungry for the same prey, both chasing the other off their kills with equal frequency. In the bigger picture of wilderness, they are partners, each alerting the other to the source of meat. They keep each other "on their toes", so to speak, contributing to a high degree of vigilance and athleticism in both species. There is nothing narcissistic or dysfunctional about them at all. In fact, they are a vital component of the wilderness. As for their human-like qualities, would it not be more colourful to expect something along the lines of what the African poet and medicine man Credo Mutwa wrote in his praise song to the *impisi*, the Zulu name for the spotted warrior of the night – the hyena?

> You are the impisi that
> pieces together the assegais
> of our forefathers.
> You are the living broom
> of our great-grandmothers ...
> You, impisi, are the friend
> of the warriors
> and those who walk
> through the night.

These words, too, are projections, but there is no doubt about the sense of partnership in this poem. Embodying the "noble" part of ourselves, Mutwa leaves us with a sense of respect and reverence for these animals. Thank you for that, Credo.

And what about the snake, that age-old serpent from Eden? Wrapped around the Tree of Life, that first chapter of Genesis makes it very clear that snakes exist on an axis of evil. But let's take another look at these remarkable reptiles.

Snakes are among the oldest of the living species on Earth. They have been around close on 150 million years. Their scales precede the evolutionary leap of feathers, the softened forms of their reptilian skin, and they grow by repeatedly shedding their skins. The symbolic significance of their capacity to outgrow their skins was not lost on the ancient Greeks. It became a powerful symbol for the teachings of the god of healing, Aesclepius, who believed that a willingness to change, to outgrow old attitudes and to become conscious of one's suffering, was essential to the healing process. Now, wrapped around the legendary staff of this great son of Apollo, the image of the snake remains, to this day, the outstanding symbol of the medical profession. In this poem, called "Snake", I pay tribute to this much maligned creature:

> Would you believe me
> if I told you that the thief of fire, Prometheus
> is my other name,
> that Aesclepius is my friend
> and that I am the message on Hermes' staff?
>
> Would you believe me
> if I told you that my serpentine course
> is how the stars unfold,
> how water finds its way
> and how flames shape themselves
> on their journey back to the sun?
>
> Would you believe me
> if I told you that whenever a man
> says "Yes!" and "No!"
> something in my skin stands up
> for I have heard a soul-maker speak?
>
> Would you believe me
> if I told you for every season in a child's life
> and for every twist in your fate
> I shed my skin
> and that this is the remedy for a rigid life?

Would you believe me
if I told you that I am the shadow of Eden's God,
that to wrap myself around you
is not to constrict you but to know you
and that even a god must shed His skin?

When Hitler, prior to World War II, declared in that famous quote, "I am Germany", he clearly identified himself as being the all-good, all-seeing, all-powerful, all-knowing Führer or "Father" of Germany. In that moment of supreme grandiosity he confirmed that he had risen above any need to acknowledge his own flawed humanity – his dark side. And so, what he could not tolerate in himself was projected and acted out in the form of a xenophobic storm aimed at Jews, Gypsies, anyone non-Aryan and, in the long run, anyone not like him. He believed this to be in the interests of his country and many other people believed it too. He certainly did not believe that he was evil.

We need to remember that power and paranoia go hand in hand. Power is an archetype geared for dominance and the earliest signs of having identified with it is an intolerance of criticism. Our projections are always emotionally charged and when we are stuck in them, what usually happens is that we begin to perceive the world in terms of ideals and absolutes. Unaware that we are doing it, we become blind not only to the objective nature of the other, particularly those onto whom our own shadow issues are targeted, but, like Dr Jekyll, they cause us to hold unrealistic expectations of ourselves.

Projections are at the heart of fanatical thinking and they play right into the hands of powerful biological strategies of personal survival – be nice to the in-group, be cool, if not nasty, to the out-group. It is easy to point fingers and to ask questions about evil demagogues. It is not that easy to face up to our own complacency, ignorance or indifference to the suffering of others. I think we need to be very careful about defining the role of others along an axis of evil. It is very easy to speak about another country's weapons of destruction and our weapons for peace, of our principles versus the fanaticism of the other, of our needs versus someone else's greed.

The shadow is archetypal. It is huge, emotionally charged and, as we have seen, potentially destructive. But it can also be creative, albeit in an unfocused sort of way. It is essential therefore that we become a lot more aware of it. Our task is to acknowledge the "beast", at the same time learning how to harness its vitality, its emotion and its raw power with an intelligence that knows how to say yes and no to it. It must not be underestimated, says Lyall Watson, but it should not be given any more credit than it deserves, either. "Together we become formidable," he says, or as Jung wrote, "we become whole". "How can I be substantial," Jung asked, "if I fail to cast a shadow? I must have a dark side also, if I am to be whole; and in as much as I become conscious of my shadow, I also remember that I am a human being like any other." Putting it another way, he once asked: "But what if I should discover that the very enemy is within me, that I myself am the enemy who must be loved ... what then?"

It is in this light that we should not be surprised to discover that the shadow of our Judeo-Christian-Abrahamic teachings is both long and dark and that its negative impact on the natural world has been profound. For everything that is valuable about the teachings of these great religions, it is nevertheless essential that we do not shy away from examining that shadow. By facing up to it, we may discover that something in us is beginning to shed its skin.

In April 1970, a landmark symposium was held in Claremont, California. Entitled "The Theology of Survival", it was a challenge to the teachings of conventional theology, more especially its contribution to the environmental crises of our time. The analyst Edward Whitmont, in his book *Psyche and Substance*, summed up the proceedings thus:

> ...it was generally agreed that the traditional Christian attitudes of the Old and New Testaments, namely, the rejection of the pagan belief in the divinity of nature and the consequent designation of man as the centre, with all

nature subservient to him, had significantly contributed to overpopulation, air and water pollution, and other ecological threats. By emphasising the value of nature only as it contributes to man's welfare, traditional theologies had tended to create an absolute gulf between man and nature.

We have paid a huge psychological price for the rejection of our so-called pagan beliefs – a price that can be readily translated as a loss of soul. As the entomologist, socio-biologist and Pulitzer winning author E O Wilson says, this rejection "has caused the spirits our ancestors knew intimately, to flee the rocks and the trees and then the distant mountains. They are now in the stars, where their final extinction is possible but improbable."

We cannot escape our Western cultural roots and neither should we, for we are steeped in its values. In other words, it is not my intention to encourage a return to paganism, animism, or to the ancient doctrines of pantheism, which is the worship of many gods. Instead, I support the attitude of the Kalahari "bushmen" who remind us that all the animals say ONE thing – we are inseparable. However, I want to honour the legend of Pan, for that legend will not go away.

Pan was the pagan god of the woods and fields. A wild, irrational deity with the horns and hooves of a goat, he was believed to evoke sudden fear in solitary travellers in the wilderness, hence the origin of the word "panic". And yet, in spite of his frightful qualities, Pan was also seen in a playful and positive light. He loved to play the pipes, also called the panpipes, and the nymphs who inhabited trees, streams and caves were said to be his partners in dance. The embodiment of the eternal spirit of youth, he eventually came to be regarded as the representative of paganism and the personification of all Nature.

The name Pan literally means "all" and because pantheism was a doctrine that denied the existence of God as a personality in favour of God as an expression of Nature, it is easy to see why it was to become the enemy of a monotheistic Judeo-Christian church that was anxious to replace it with the teachings of an invisible, masculine God and in whose image we alone, the human animal, are made.

As the story goes, it is said that at the time of Christ's birth, a mysterious voice was heard in the Greek Isles announcing that the great Pan was dead. The battle lines between the teachings of those who believed in the soul of Nature and those who believed in the spirit of an invisible, monotheistic God, had not only been drawn, but a victory for the latter proclaimed.

And then came the Nicene Creed. A little over a thousand years ago, in the year 869, in the ancient city of Constantinople the all-male Principals of the Holy Catholic Church finalised what we know today as the Nicene Creed – the formal and final statement of the chief tenets of Christian belief as adopted by a previous Council in the city of Nicaea eighty-two years previously. On that day, at that meeting in Constantinople, says the psychologist and writer James Hillman, soul finally lost its dominion. "Our notion of a tripartite cosmos of spirit, soul and body, devolved into a dualism of spirit (or mind) and body (or matter)." Soul as an image of depth, darkness, warmth, moistness and animation, in short – creativity and femininity – was displaced, or rather, incorporated into the more masculine-orientated notion of spirit. Hillman continues ... "What the Constantinople Council did to soul, rejecting this image, only culminated a long process beginning with Paul, the Saint, of substituting and disguising, and, forever after, confusing soul with spirit."

Spirit and soul are not the same. Like the rows of thorns on the ziziphus, they anticipate each other. They are complementary opposites. Spirit is cool, pointed and soaring. It gives us wings. Soul is Earth-bound and warm. It gives us roots. It loves the Earth and everything that comes out of it. Soul knows about the shadow. And as anyone involved in healing will tell you, the wounds of the spirit are most often healed by soul.

In the psyche as it is in the world "out there", what we subdue, deny and dominate comes back to us – if we let it. If we don't it comes back at us. It is evident, in spite of the Nicene Creed and the long history of attempts to negate the pagan belief in animal deities, the image and influence of animals in the human psyche refuse to go away. As the biblical scholar Charbonneau Lassay wrote,

> Our unconscious bond with animals might explain why the fantastic stories of animals, birds and trees brought back to the West by the first great world travellers of the second half of the Middle Ages were so rapidly taken over by the Western symbolists to represent the gifts of God and even Christ himself.

It may also explain the shared and troubled visions of the seventh century Hebrew prophet Ezekiel and the evangelist St. John, both of whom saw the coming to life of four animals in the mysterious crown of Christ:

> ... and the first beast was like a lion and the second beast like a calf, and the third beast had the face of a man and the fourth beast was like a flying eagle. And they were saying holy, holy, holy – which was and is and is to come.

Is it any wonder that these visionaries were troubled? Is it any wonder that we have established societies to prevent cruelty to these creatures – these second-class citizens of human society? And is it too much to suppose that the core of the modern feminist as well as the environmental movements of our day are the inevitable psychological rebellion against the long-standing negation and oppression of soul?

When the great myth of Pan is reviewed, it should become clear that the pagan god of the wild did not die at all. Instead, he went underground. His hiding place, for the past two thousand years, has been in the shadowy depths of the human psyche. Psychologically, the death of Pan can be interpreted as the repression of the instinctive, spontaneous, raw or wild parts of the psyche that occurred with the rise of a monotheistic consciousness. Great Pan did not really die, however, for nothing in the psyche dies. Like molecular particles, which can be changed but not destroyed, ideas can be repressed, yes, but extinguished ... no.

It is well known, in analytical work, that that which we reject we project, and in this light, says the social scientist and naturalist Herbert Schroeder, it is no wonder that the horned and hoofed image of Pan was so easily incorporated into the Christian mythology of Satan. This tells us that when a natural archetype such as Pan is repressed, it becomes part of our shadow, only to reappear in a negative form outside of us, as the great enemy, a source of danger, suffering and evil. In the case of Pan, however, the inner psychic struggle between instinct and consciousness, between our biology and what we might become, was then projected beyond the concept of Satan to the outer world of soul and Nature – the playing fields of Pan. What ensued has been an ongoing, archetypal battle between Light and Darkness, with wild nature, including the wild parts of ourselves, cast in the role of Darkness, a phenomenon to be conquered, civilised and subdued.

The history of colonialism bears testimony to this claim, an example of which is the 1492 "discovery" of America by Columbus, the same year that Jews, by royal edict, were evicted from Spain. Barry Lopez writes: "...a process was set in motion that would lead to the incredible sixteenth-century atrocities by the conquistadors against the natives of the New World." It was against those who lived close to Nature and to the animals. These atrocities were not confined to the Americas, by the way, but to almost every country where indigenous people were deemed by those who colonised them to be heathen, pagan and in need of conversion to *their* way of thinking and to *their* notions of Nature and of God.

And what about the notion of Man as the apex of creation? A clue as to the perpetuation of this inflated belief can be found in the twenty-eighth verse of the first chapter of Genesis: be fruitful and multiply and replenish the Earth and subdue it: and have dominion over the fish of the sea and over the fowl of the air, and over every living thing that moveth upon the face of the Earth.

At great cost, not only to ourselves but to the environment, we have taken this admonition all too literally. Looked at critically, it can be seen as an admonition for survival, and not without profound, biological undertones either. It tells us that the enemy is "out there", that we are the in-group, the champions, the blessed and the inheritors of the Earth. It has played right into our genetically driven needs for territory, rank, status, security, esteem, attachment and belonging – us versus them. Inevitably, it has reinforced the inflated belief that human beings are at the cutting edge of creation. But it has done more. It has defined the "other" as different, to be subdued and therefore lesser than us. We have tended to regard the importance of "every living thing that moveth upon the Earth" not according to the intrinsic worth of all living things, but according to how useful they are to us. We have forgotten not only the meaning we derive from them, but more importantly, the profound influence they have in our lives as soul-makers.

If there was indeed a voice from the Greek Isles announcing that the great Pan was dead, how different is it from that of the eighteenth-century philosopher Nietzsche (1844–1900) who, in his book *Joyous Wisdom*, shockingly announced, "God is dead!" What did he mean and, in the light of an ecological intelligence, what – if anything – is its significance? Could it be that the voice of Pan is being heard once more, this time in the psyche of the human animal, telling us that the animals are within us, that every living thing is an expression of God and that we are the keepers of our zoo? For me, the analyst Edward Edinger answers this question beautifully: "God has fallen out of heaven, and into the psyche of man. Each individual is now obliged to find his or her own unique relation to the numinosum." In other words, each individual must find his or her own relationship to the religious experience. Then there is the writer Thomas Elsner, who sees the "death of God" as the beginning of individuation in Jung's sense of the word, and also the beginning of a process of transformation and a renewal of the God-image itself. The "death of God" then, is the shedding of a skin.

It is time to shed our prejudices against things that are wild, untamed or unconverted – more especially our animal nature. Historically, almost every animal – from the fabulous beasts, the phoenix, sphinx and centaur, to birds, sea creatures, insects and domestic animals – has, in some way, struck a cord in the human psyche. How can we forget them? They are on our family crests and they are in our dreams. More than forty constellations in the southern night sky are named after them and every second sports team has its animal totem. In any modern home there is bound to be a picture, a painting or a calendar that features some kind of non-human animal. We have toy animals, animal carvings and animal stories. They are in our blood and in our imagination. And now, with the unravelling of the human genome, we have proof of a kinship of science and soul. And let's not forget those animals that rarely feature on our family crests – hyenas, vultures and the other shadow animals in our psyche. Let's welcome them back again. After all, we named them. They, too, are our soul mates and we can learn a lot about ourselves from them. Life without animals would be unthinkable. It is what the poets and the shamans have been trying to tell us for years. Let's remember our wild side.

So you see, if you fall into a lion's pit the reason the lion will tear you to pieces is not because it's hungry or because it's bloodthirsty ... but because you've invaded its territory.

Yann Martel – The Life Of Pi

One of the biggest intellectual challenges of the 21st century will be to construct unified images of human nature that do not denigrate our animal past or our future potentials as members of the human family.

Jaak Panskepp

5

REMEMBERING OUR WILD SIDE

A SPECTACULAR EVENT WHICH SUDDENLY SURPASSES THE GREAT NEWS STORIES OF THE WORLD: OUR FATHER, NORMALLY A WORRIED AND SERIOUS MAN, DOES AN UNDERWATER HANDSTAND IN THE BAY.

© MICHAEL LEUNIG

Leunig

I N A WORLD THAT GENERALLY REGARDS REFINEMENT AND DOMESTICATION OF everything from sugar to human instincts to be the hallmarks of civilisation and progress, we need to be mindful that invariably something significant has been lost in the process. Civilisation, for all its so-called advances and advantages, has cost many of us, perhaps too many, our sense of wildness. Sometimes we are not even sure what this wildness means, but it does not take much analysis to realise that deep down, we really miss it.

To be wild is to be alert to the needs of the flesh and the warning calls of distress. It is to be spontaneous – to *live* one's Earthiness and one's notions of God independent of outside approval. It is to dance, to work and to play with passion and, when called upon, to act dispassionately, swiftly and without personal feeling or bias. It is to be as patient as a heron – to be able to wait for hours at the edge of hunger. It is to understand the double meaning of the word outrageous – to act *without* rage, to do something out of character, to cross-dress, to stilt walk to a disciplinary hearing, to use a shoe as a basketball and to make a fool of yourself without being stupid. Its other meaning is to act *out of rage*. It is to be aware of the fury at the edge of an "inner" hurricane and to know your way back to the calmness at its eye. It is to conform every now and then, also to be streetwise and to be unafraid of entering those inner and outer territories where shit happens. It is the man-child, woman-child in us that admires this kind of wildness in others, especially in our fathers and mothers. It is that same child that loves the wildness of nudity, who longs for a larynx that is free to sing and shout and who loves to go down to the river and to watch it as if she was watching the flow of her own blood.

The poet Robert Bly reminds us that the wildness of the wild man is neither criminal nor psychotic. Rather, as Yeats puts it, it is to be "mad as the mist and snow". And we do miss that madness. How many of us remember, sometimes with nostalgia, sometimes with envy, the wild, benign mischief-makers of our youth so aptly described by Rumi in this poem, translated by Coleman Barks and John Moyne: "Has anyone seen the boy?"

> Has anyone seen the boy who used to come here?
> Round-faced troublemaker, quick to find a joke,
> slow to be serious, red shirt,
> perfect co-ordination, sly, strong muscled,
> with things always in his pocket: reed flute,
> worn pick, polished and ready for his Talent
> you know that one.
> Have you heard stories about him?
> Pharaoh and the whole Egyptian world
> collapsed for such a Joseph.

> I'd gladly spend years getting word
> of him, even third or fourth hand.

Children love the wild anecdotes of their parents. Porous to the psychic conditions that surround them, they love the hidden stories of the soul, often demanding to hear them again and again. It is a strange fact that children often grow up to become the champions of the unlived wildness of their parents. These children are sometimes known as the black sheep of our families.

And then there is Rilke who, in this masterful poem, writes of the caged wildness of the panther in all of us:

> His vision, from the constantly passing bars,
> has grown so weary, that it cannot hold anything else.
> It seems to him that there are a thousand bars,
> and behind the bars, no world.
>
> As he paces in cramped circles, over and over,
> the movement of his powerful, soft strides
> is like a ritual dance around a centre
> in which a mighty will stands ... paralysed.
> Only at times,
> only at times ... the curtain of the pupil lifts ...
> quietly an image enters in,
> rushes down through the tense, arrested muscles,
> plunges into the heart
> and is gone.

I think we can all, in some small way, relate to the "stuckness" of that elegant yet pathetic animal in the poem. We are the only animal who can turn our back on our animal nature and it is then, and precisely then, that the bars come down on our world. To be caged is another way of describing a loss of creativity. Watch out for it. It is a well-known condition among all men and women who "go to work". It is called burn out

– a condition in which the sensing of the dream of what one always wanted to do or to be enters one's thoughts, plunges into the heart and disappears. It is about a career that began as a passion, then became a duty and, finally, a burden. Be aware of the process, for in its early stages, the signs are subtle. You will hear it in the sharpened cynicism of your speech when you talk about your work. You will feel it in the growing heaviness of your body when the subject of work is raised. Because our identity is so intimately linked with our work, and with it "the complex, volatile chemistry of approval, self-worth and the instinct to provide", says the poet David Whyte, it is vital that you keep asking yourself, "What has become of me in my work?"

Creativity, passion and vision invariably go together, which is why Rilke's poem of the panther is so significant. Try not to forget the vision, the energy and the wild archetype – that great inner artist that drew you into your work in the first place. Try to remember who, or what, put you behind those bars, if not you? After all, said Camus "a man's work is nothing but a slow trek to rediscover, through the detours of art, those two or three great and simple images in whose presence his heart first opened".

To lose touch with one's wildness is to mistake it for brutality – the shadow, or the dark side of wildness. As Bly confirms, "some boys are so afraid of becoming domesticated that they become savage". They become defiant, aggressive, coarse and self-destructive – the very opposite of the wildness that we miss. And as many of us know, there is sometimes a fine line between what is savage and what is wild. The poet Theodore Roethke captures the knife-edged fineness of the line – as well as the fear of what could be unleashed when it is crossed. In his poem, "Papa's Waltz" it can be found in his description of the face of a mother watching her husband, lost in a drunken dance with their young son.

> We romped until the pans
> Slid from the kitchen shelf;
> My mother's countenance
> Could not unfrown itself.

HUMAN SURVIVAL – WILD STRATEGIES

From bacteria to buffalos and boffins, the history of everything organic can be described by the British science-educator Michael Poole's acronym MR GREEN, which stands for movement, respiration, growth, reproduction, excitability, excretion and nutrition. It is at the same time a history of self preservation and protection, involving competition, challenge, cooperation, collaboration, opportunism, deception, risk taking and even altruism. It does not matter who or where we are, our lives at all times will involve subtle and sometimes obvious combinations of these survival strategies. Whether we are lions, hyenas or humans, we engage in these activities for the same reasons – for food, turf or territory, for security, for approval, for sexual partners, for rank, status, attachment and belonging. And our emotions and residual feelings come along with them – anticipatory pleasure, anxiety, fear, joy, disappointment, envy, hate, frustration, panic, distress, contentment and love. In the interest of self-preservation we employ these strategies not only to establish ourselves, but also to promote and to protect ourselves. This is nothing to be ashamed of. For example, cooperation – that essential social endeavour to share one's life with another, is, at its roots, an endeavour to enhance one's own protection and survival.

It is difficult to find a creature that is not equipped with some form of self-protection. From the exoskeletons of beetles, tortoises and lobsters, from stings, thorns and claws, to the burglar bars, jagged written warnings and barbed words of human speech, every organism has a way of dealing with external threats to its existence. Every creature is, in some way, geared to being sensitive to and of escaping from danger. Some organisms rely on speed or brute strength to protect themselves, others on electro-chemical defences such as toxic juices and repellent sprays. And that includes the human animal. How many of us live in homes surrounded by electric fences or have been on the stinging end of an accusation designed to shock? Attacking language is a part of the evolution of the human tongue and so is the socially expedient ability to say, "I'm sorry".

When they are balanced, our survival strategies are healthy – they hold families, units, teams, societies and civilisations together. On the other hand, any excessive or under use of any one of them is a guarantee for individual or group disharmony often presenting as frustration, withdrawal, isolation, anger, passive aggression and depression – some of the reasons why people seek psychological help.

Because it is such an integral part of our shadow, the strategy that we are least likely to own up to is deception. Deception is an ancient game in which the human animal is an expert. Its roots are biological and wild. Take, for instance, the Red-winged Pratincole, *Glareola pratincola*, which pretends to have a broken wing in order to divert the attention of an egg-seeking predator away from its nest and towards itself. Do we do that? Absolutely. We are the great pretenders. We pretend not so much with broken "wings" but with broken words – we mislead, mimic and misinform, which is why it is almost impossible for us to be "transparent". To be accountable, yes … but to be transparent, no. And it is not about being dishonest. We all have skeletons in our cupboards and sometimes that's exactly where they should remain. We all have dreams and schemes and to make them known prematurely is sometimes to put an end to them altogether. If it directly affects me, I might not want to know your secrets and you, for the same reason, might not want to know mine. In other words, it is one thing to have all of one's cards on the table, so to speak – to be accountable – but it is another to have them all turned up at the same time. We might not be ready for what we want to find out, for as the Russian writer and Soviet dissident Varlam Shalamov, wrote after seventeen years in a Siberian prison, "There is much that a man should not know, should not see, and if he does see it, it is better to die." And then there is the poet Czeslaw Milosz who writes:

No-one with
Impunity gives himself the eyes of a god.

True deception, writes the primatologist Frans De Waal, "is one of those capacities that we employ all the time without taking too much pride in it. It can be defined as the deliberate projection, to one's own advantage, of a false image of past behaviour, knowledge, or intention. In its most complete sense, it requires awareness of how one's actions come across and what the outside world is likely to read into them."

We are indeed the great pretenders, masters at disguising our emotions and our intentions. We are also the masters of *self-deception*. We pretend to be what we are not, deluding ourselves into believing that we are the apex of creation, intrinsically different to other animals, the inheritors of the Earth, the masters of our fate. And when things go wrong with our stewardship we pretend that we did not know, or we twist the truth. Struggling to distance ourselves from our animal nature, we tend to believe that the virtues of courage, patience, fair play and moderation are the sole property of *Homo sapiens* and if we do happen to recognise these qualities in wolves, elephants, baboons, cats and dogs, then we are accused of anthropomorphism. Deception can be expedient and therefore necessary, but it can also be sinister. The philosopher Nietzsche, for instance, believed that some of the virtues we most admire in others such as prudence, sympathy and delayed gratification are sublimations of motives that we readily condemn, such as cruelty, cunning, resentment and revenge.

In social settings, especially if it involves the harmony of an in-group, it is often inexpedient to be brutally honest. Discretion is the better part of valour, we are told, and so, in order to keep the peace, we learn to remain silent, to tell "white-lies" and half-truths. We all know how to "cry wolf" and the monkeys are our genetic mentors. Watch a vervet monkey, *Cercopithecus aethiops*, harassed by its companions and it won't take long before it utters a false cry of warning that there is a leopard, a raptor or a snake nearby. This, of course, sends the harassing monkeys scattering for safety. As it is with humans, these false calls of alarm are not taken lightly by the troop and they are effective, provided they are not continually misused. Young vervets, not unlike young children, spend a lot of time practising the different alarm calls – with minimal response from the adults.

Like the vervets, we too have learned the art of distraction. We all have our hard-luck stories and we all fall for them. We have all been conned and we all have something of the conman in us. When will we ever learn? The likely answer, especially if it involves the possibility of some form of reward, is never. And we are not shy to maximise our strong points either, to exaggerate or to put ourselves in a positive light, and as for minimising our negative aspects, who of us is genuinely enthusiastic about displaying the photographs in our passports or on our driving licences?

Am I being too hard or too cynical about the human animal? Perhaps I am, but I don't want to be too soft either. If it makes us feel a little better about ourselves, let's try to understand deception as a strategy that is often not only individually and socially expedient, but also necessary. On the other hand, let's not confuse deception with a disregard for accountability. What is important is that we learn to become conscious of our survival strategies – why and when we are employing them. We have to put them to the test from time to time. Are they appropriate, are they acceptable, are they meaningful and, finally, are they flexible?

E volved to communicate information and purpose, one of the most important of the survival skills of all living creatures is language. In other words, it includes, but is not confined to, the syntax and symbols of human speech. Broadly defined, language is a system whereby different species through the communication and receiving of information coordinate their activities. When looked at a little more closely, almost everything, from mathematics, music and landscape to dreams and spider webs, is a carrier of information. This information has to be perceived, interpreted and, if necessary, acted upon.

Compared with other animals, the human sensory equipment is nothing to boast about. For example, when it comes to auditory perception, one very quickly discovers just how limited our range of hearing actually is. The human auditory system is receptive to sounds between 20 Hz and 20,000 Hz where one Hertz (Hz) is equivalent to one wave or vibration of sound in one second. Dogs can hear up to about 45,000 Hz. Cats, including the big ones, go even higher – 85,000 Hz. Bats and dolphins are the likely high-frequency champions among mammals, detecting sounds as high as 100,000 Hz. But even they cannot compare with insects such as moths, which can hear sounds at 240,000 Hz. Then there is infrasound. Way below the human limit, elephants can vocalise at 8Hz. The significance of this low-frequency communication in elephants is that these great animals can keep in touch with each other over distances up to 300 kilometres! No wonder these animals are scarce when the hunters are around.

For every creature capable of vocalisation, the sounds they utter are likely to be one or more of the following: contact, alarm, territorial, separation, sexual, comfort or safety calls. It is what the linguist Derek Bickerton, refers to as proto-language rather than full language where the former is primarily a communication system, with the latter having a mapping function – a means of representing the world internally. If proto-language is primarily a system of communicating the emotions of fear, desire, anger and triumph etc, then it is a language that is still very much with us. It is in the tone of our voices, the timing of our speech and of our outbursts and in that subtle and – sometimes – not so subtle phenomenon called body language. The human face, for instance, is capable of seven thousand different expressions, each a different way of communicating with others. Facial and body language accounts for an astonishing seventy-five percent of the information we communicate – and that's without having said a word.

The contact calls of birds, wild dogs and lions, for example, are as unmistakable as ours. "Here I am ...where are you?" is Konrad Lorenz's classical interpretation of the contact calls of animals. Their whoops, grunts and twitters are no less significant than our "hello", "good morning", "it's good to see you" and "how are you?" "Watch out!" is the message of an alarm call in any language and until recently it was believed that humans were the only creatures who could differentiate what it is that one needs to watch out for. Birds, for instance, were believed to have non-specific alarm calls, but Dr Chris Evans of MacQuarie University in Sydney challenged this perception. Querying our notions of these so-called "birdbrains", his work has shown that our domestic chickens, through separate utterances, "squawk" the difference between raptors and ground predators. The squirrel-like suricates, *Suricata suricatta*, on the other hand, mimic the calls of eagles, jackals and snakes to warn their companions of these particular enemies. Then there are Africa's green monkeys, the vervets, who are known to have at least sixty different information calls which include, as already mentioned, specific alarm calls for leopards, raptors and snakes. The same goes for elephants. Joyce Poole, who has spent more than twenty-five years in the Amboseli National Park in Kenya studying these great animals, believes they employ up to seventy different vocalisations, many of them sub-sonic, and which they use in different contexts. Not only that – it is believed, in the same way that we are called by our personal names, they have specific calls for specific members within their groups. Then there is the lion whose alarm calls vary from a short cough, to a "huh" or a hiss. We don't know yet, but it is likely that these separate calls could also be specific.

When it comes to the language of territory and turf, the human animal compares well with our evolutionary brothers and sisters. Territory, to have one's piece of land, is an instinct, as the great novelist John Steinbeck wrote, and don't we know it? Signs such as "trespassers will be prosecuted", "beware of the dog," and "this property is patrolled by armed response" are not merely human inventions. We might as well be talking about lions whose territorial sprays and roars say the same thing ... "this land is mine ... mine ... mine". And then there are the hoops and sprays of the spotted hyena, who cries back at the lion, "oh no ... it isn't". Our signatures of ownership and territory are found not only on title deeds, but in the tracks we leave in and around our own households. They are the wet towels we leave lying on the bed and the scattered clothing on the floor. Is this adolescent laziness or do we unconsciously do it as a signal to show we have been there or that this room is mine ... mine ...mine?

Spoken language is far more than just words or sounds. It is the way that sounds and words are used that makes this form of communication the powerful survival tool that it is. Tone, rhythm and pitch all play a vital part when it comes to the accurate communication of attitudes, needs and circumstance. As with the human animal, lions too are sensitive to the significance of the graded roars, meows, growls, snarls and grunting calls of their colleagues. Changing the volume, intensity, tempo and tone of the call, writes Richard Estes in his informative *Behaviour Guide to African Mammals*, allows lions to express a wide range of emotions. Closer to home, the relaxed chatter of baboons and birds is not unlike the banter of the human animal, a profoundly important contact strategy of social animals, significant not only for its soothing effect but for that moment when everything suddenly goes quiet.

The language of the wild is not limited to cries and calls either. It includes a sophisticated "body" language in the form of long-lasting pheromones in pastes, excretions, secretions and sprays – activities designed to communicate territory, rank, hormonal status, sexual readiness and general intra-species information. It is also a way of asking, "Where are the neighbours?" Brown hyenas, *Hyaena brunnea*, for example, exude two types of paste: a long-lasting one used for territorial marking, and a short-lasting one for passing on information to other members of the resident clan. Brown hyenas are social creatures but they forage alone, covering vast distances each night in search of carrion, pasting scent-marks two to three times in every kilometre. This has led Dr Gus Mills, a renowned expert on the hyenas of the Kalahari, to suspect that the short-acting paste is to inform other members of the clan that the area has already been searched for food.

Connected to the nasal passages but situated behind the front incisors is an active gland, common to most animals, that acts as a receptor for picking up airborne chemicals or pheromones. Through the use of this gland, they can interpret the sexual status and readiness of potential breeders. The male greater kudu, *Tragelaphus strepsiceros*, for instance, can scent the sexual pheromones of in-season females up to ten kilometres away. Known as Jacobson's gland, it is non-functioning in humans, but it has left its evolutionary imprint – it occasionally flares up in children, presenting as an inflamed cyst behind the upper two incisors. We too have our pheromones naturally, and in deodorants and perfumes. Backed up by evocative labels and brand names, the sexual signals are unmistakable. Human scenting and scent marking cannot be divorced from our animal origins and as for the marking of one's territory, which self-respecting male, not without a sigh of satisfaction, does not enjoy the occasional marking of his own garden in the old-fashioned way? Our territorial signatures are everywhere, from our homes and gardens to the graffiti on subway walls and in the passive aggression of litter.

Plants, too, have their language – their way of saying yes and no and they do it in a measurable way. An example of this is the chemical "communication" between Africa's great thorn trees, the acacias, and the animals that browse on them. In response to the meal-time assault, the acacias, by pushing tannic acid from the stems into the leaves, quickly elevate the tannin levels in the foliage to unpalatable proportions. This gives the browsers such as giraffes and kudu about ten to twenty minutes to make the most of their leafy meal, after which they have to move on. But there is more. The tannin warning is not limited to the animal browsers alone. The same tannins have a pheromone component that is carried downwind, informing other acacias of the impending assault, thus stimulating tannin secretions into the leaves of the unbrowsed trees. The acacias, like the animals that browse on them, also keep in touch with each other and the reason is the same – survival. But what about the survival of the giraffes and the kudu? It should not be surprising to know that these animals have learned not only to spread themselves out while they are browsing but also to browse upwind.

Then there is speech, the gift or talent we would surely regard as that which most distinguishes us not only from the rest of the animal kingdom but also from our hominin forefathers. Our spoken language deserves a rethink, for it involves a lot more than the development of an athletic tongue. The evolution of two asymmetrical hemispheres, with one of them, usually the left hemisphere (in eighty to ninety percent of us), housing the all-important integrating and executive centres for human speech. It has been a major milestone in our evolution. It has been as crucial for our survival as a species as was the harnessing of fire. Our earliest words, sentences and then our stories, became the kindling that kept the early fires of human consciousness alive. Bickerton might agree with this, for he goes as far as to say that it is language, because it dominates all aspects of human cerebral function, rather than intelligence, that defines *Homo sapiens*.

Through spoken language we can articulate memories, we can announce the signs of the times, we can speak our thoughts, and more – we can conceptualise and talk *about* things. It is an ego skill that functions not as some kind of neuro-anatomical switch that can be turned on and off, but rather it is a widespread, cerebral system involved in the processing, organising and imparting of information, both external and internal. According to many psychologists, one's true sense of individuality would not have developed in the absence of a spoken language. Inherent in the noun-verb structure of our speech comes the inevitable differentiation between the subject and the object and, with it, the reinforcing of "I", "me" and "you". Indeed, says the British neuro-psychiatrist TJ Crow, who believes that schizophrenia, world-wide, is associated with impaired hemispheric dominance for speech, "it is difficult to imagine that an individual could contemplate the world, develop ideas, delusional or otherwise, or the capacity for rational thought, without language."

The sheer depth of our vocabulary and the capacity to use it has set us apart from our hominin ancestors. Hungry for news and information about our world, speech has sharpened our intellect. Its role in human relationships cannot be underestimated, for we bond, we gossip and we groom each other with words. To hear one's language and dialect in a foreign country is to feel a surge of soul. It is a homecoming. And yet, words are a part of our undoing, for they can have a cutting edge. Sometimes we wound each other with words: we talk too much, and we say things we do not mean.

And then there is the poem "Echo" from *Wild Gifts* that seeks the I and thou of co-existence...

> I can only speak for myself
> and then, not always so
> for how much of you and him and her
> do I echo?

> And the mountains and the streams
> and the sea
> do I speak for you
> or is it you that speaks
> for me?

> And the eagle, the mantis
> and the trees
> do you live your lives in the wild
> out there
> or in the wild
> in me?

> I can only speak for myself
> when I hear your echo in me
> when I hear my lion call in you
> and your eagle cry in me.

When we listen to the wind, the streams and the calls of the birds and animals, our spoken language with its vowels, consonants and syllables can easily be appreciated as a deeply rooted harnessing of the clicks, the calls, the cries, the groans and the breath sounds of the wild. Sadly, we have forgotten the origins of our wild tongue. We have forgotten that every time we speak, our wild history is on show and that the alphabet – the building blocks of written language and with it, the capacity to read and write, is a gift from the forests, the sea and the animals. Even reading and writing can be seen as a sophisticated form of the ancient "writing" and reading of tracks.

In what way have the themes or topics of modern-day conversation differed from those of our hominin ancestors? The answer, it would seem, is very little. It was Jung who remarked that the origins of directive thinking coincided with the origins of spoken language. He saw our earliest speech as the first stirrings of a cry to our companions that water has been found, or that a bear has killed or been killed, or that a storm is approaching, or that wolves are prowling around the camp. It would appear that the daily information we exchange with our companions today is, in many respects, simple and sophisticated variations of these themes. "We have found water" is a statement charged with excitement, relief, joy, security, triumph and homecoming. It tells us that we have found what we were looking for. The corporate goal has been reached. For the time being we have struck gold, oil, meat or material wealth. We can rest a while, we can gossip and we can reflect. To find water is to have succeeded, to have struck form. Psychologically, it is to find oneself in the flow of things, perhaps to have discovered a wellspring, a place of potential depth or meaning in one's life, or a space where one can lick one's psychological wounds.

"The bear has been killed" is a message of multiple meanings. It could be telling us that danger has been averted, that the struggle is over, that a cycle has completed itself and that we can begin anew. It might come with undertones of excitement, relief and surprise, but a kill is also a killing. Who did it? What's in it for us? Will it be shared? Will there be more killings? These are familiar corporate boardroom questions, aren't they? The bear, then, could be a hero or a villain, the central character in a scandal or even a scapegoat.

"There is a storm approaching." Be careful. Be aware. Be vigilant. Make the proper preparations. This might not be a good time to hunt or to take a holiday. Make sure the pantry is stocked. Change is coming. The storms are also the socio-political storms on our horizons. Perhaps it is a good time to move to higher ground, or to leave the country. For some, the storm is overdue and it is a good time to stay. Like modern day stockbrokers, our ancestors were interpreting the signs of the times.

Then there are the prowling wolves, the troubles close to home, the brewing storms that were once on the horizons and which we thought would go away but are suddenly upon us. These are the storms of the psyche, the ones which we know we have to face, that must not be avoided, says DH Lawrence in these lines from the poem "The Song Of A Man Who Has Come Through":

> ... what is the knocking at the door in the night?
> It is somebody wants to do us harm.
> No, no, it is the three strange angels.
> Admit them, admit them.

The capacity for reflective thinking, for analysis, and symbol formation is largely the domain of the human animal but it is not limited to humans. It is well known that chimpanzees and bonobos have mastered symbolic thought, albeit on a limited level. For example, they have learned to use long, thin sticks as tools to "fish" termites out of their mounds. Such use of tools is not confined to our primate cousins either, for elephants are tool users as well. I have personally witnessed a Namibian desert elephant picking up a long stick and using it not only to scratch its abdomen but, in the same grooming session, to scratch behind its ear as well, before discarding it.

Our inner world of words appears to be an ongoing silent and sometimes not-so-silent dialogue of questions and answers. Do this, don't do that. What if this, what if that? Ought I, or ought I not? Our speech, a cohesion of syntax, semantics and symbols, has been crucial for our survival as a species of perennial problem solvers. Our thoughts in the form of silent and not-so-silent words take wings, for we talk to God, whatever our notions of God may be, we talk to absent loved ones, to the landscape and to animals and sometimes we could swear that they talk to us too. Even when we are asleep, the dialogue continues, this time in the form of dreams, what Freud and Jung recognised as the language of the unconscious. In our ongoing inner dialogue, who or what are we addressing? To whom are we saying yes and no and no again and yes? And who answers us? Could it be one of the three strange angels that D H Lawrence has asked us to admit – the reptile in us, that first mammal, or that two-and-a-half-million-year-old hominin survivor in the human psyche? Operating as a trio, the neurological equivalent of the strange angels can be seen as the combined functional aspects of the brainstem, the paleo-mammalian cortex and the modern human forebrain.

And then there is literacy, that great gift of the free thinker. The ability to read and write and to have a confidence that takes literacy for granted must never be underestimated. It represents a huge leap in the evolution of culture and consciousness. It allows us to read in private, to make up or own minds about what we are reading, to cross-reference our findings, to discover new words and new worlds. It takes us into the borders of other countries and into the skin of those who live there. Literacy stirs the imagination. It puts clothes on our thoughts. It extends our vocabulary and our horizons and, because it is economically and politically empowering, it is easy to see why it is the cornerstone of what we broadly refer to as a modern education.

Finally, there is ecological literacy – the ability to read the ecological issues of our time, to interpret the connections in the web of life and to recognise our evolutionary signatures within it. It is a literacy that is able to read and write with both eyes – an empirical eye that delights in science and classical reasoning and another, a poetic eye – the one that interprets the uncharted waters of non-science, that can read the future in the wind, the rain and the land. How can we tell the future from that, you might ask? I don't know. Perhaps it's the same way that the great sculptors, by staring at it, come to know the future of the block of marble in front of them. Ecological literacy is a literacy that is impossible to those who are blind to our animal nature.

When Jung proposed his notion of a collective unconscious, more especially the notion of a more than two-million-year-old hominin in all of us, I believe he was honouring the wild man, the wild woman and the wild animal in us also – our primal nature, our wild archetype.

"Every individual life is at the same time the external life of the species," he once said, implying that evolution includes the evolution of consciousness also and that the wild man and the wild woman are not very far from the surface of our domesticated social masks. If this is so, as I believe it is, I think we need to look behind us from time to time, to read the tracks of our evolutionary history and to remember where we have come from.

> Tracking
> is a gift of the wild,
> of retracing steps,
> looking back
> from time to time
> at our first spoor,
> our other signatures.

... think molecular

Norman Maclean

*Even now, I imagine that I can feel all the particles of
the universe nourishing my consciousness just as my
consciousness informs all the particles of the universe.*

Jacquetta Hawkes

6

LIVING IN A MINDFIELD

I N THIS CHAPTER I WANT TO PUSH THE ECOLOGICAL ENVELOPE. I WANT YOU
to become aware of the constant interplay between our brains, our
thoughts, our emotions, our intentions and the environment. I
wish to reinforce what the poets have known for a long time – that we
are connected to the lives of plants, planets, stars and animals in ways
that are not as mysterious as we sometimes think, or as we would sometimes like to believe.

Could it be that we are born not only into ancient fields of gravity, electricity and magnetism, but also into a "mindfield" – a field of information
in which conscious and unconscious mental activities, signals and directions interact and influence each other. Absurd? I don't think so. When we
review the evolution of life on our planet "is it that unreasonable to imagine the emergence out of our molecular origins, a continuity of geogenesis
followed by biogenesis and out of that, like a Chinese puzzle, an emerging
psychogenesis?" asks Jacquetta Hawkes. And if we acknowledge the biological continuum of anatomy and physiology (the structure and functioning of the body) then why not a continuum of the brain, the psyche
and the world around us? If this sounds plausible, then say yes quickly.

Because it concerns the subject of ecological intelligence, I want you to
be mindful of two important questions: to what degree are we receptive to
events and processes within this field of information? Secondly, to what
degree are we aware of our personal contributions into it? The answers to
these questions may not be readily forthcoming but the search for them
is what this chapter addresses.

O n 26 December 2004, an undersea earthquake north west of the
island of Sumatra resulted in the formation of a tidal wave that

would bring havoc to the coastlines of countries and islands in the Bay of Bengal. Within hours of the sudden shift of the subterranean plates, tens of thousands of people lost their lives. Millions lost their homes. It will stand as one of the greatest Human-Nature tragedies ever known. The Japanese word "tsunami" is now part of a universal language.

With reports of destruction and the rising toll of death flooding our television screens, I began to fear for the fate of the Andaman islanders, people with a stone-age culture who live under the protection of the government of India. Andaman is part of an archipelago situated very close to where the 9.3 (Richter Scale) earthquake occurred. I then began to worry about the fate of the animals, not so much for the marine creatures, but for those that lived close to the coastlines. Would they have known what was about to happen? What I subsequently learned filled me with a deep sense of relief, gratitude and respect for our wild relatives.

Yala National Park in Sri Lanka is home to at least two hundred elephants as well as a host of other large and small mammals. Its coastal boundary as well as several kilometres of inland reserve were devastated by the impact of the tsunami and yet, according to a senior official of the park, not one dead animal had been found. The elephants and other animals had moved to higher ground hours before the tsunami struck. Even if this report was not one hundred per cent accurate, clearly these animals knew of the imminent danger. How did they know? I will suggest that the elephants could feel it coming. It is known that these great pachyderms can pick up vibrations through their feet from sources over two hundred kilometres away. They probably heard it coming as well, for they can pick up sounds way below and above the human limits. For the elephants, the alarm had been sounded and it would not surprise me that the other animals, if they hadn't picked up the alarm themselves, simply joined the elephants on their trek to safety. From suricates to squirrels, baboons, leopards and francolins, animals know the alarm calls of their neighbours.

But what about the Andaman islanders? Once again, to my great relief, I learned that there were no immediate casualties. Prior to the event which would have brought certain death to those living close to the shore, they too had moved to higher ground. How did they know? Did they also hear it coming or perhaps feel it through the soles of their feet? I doubt it. While it needs confirmation, I would suggest that one reason for their escape was that they watched the behaviour of the birds and the land animals, both wild and domestic. As has been documented in the earthquake city of Santiago in Chile, the agitated behaviour of the animals probably alerted the islanders as to what was about to happen. Another reason is that these people belong to an oral culture. The stories and legends of their people are told again and again. Although the last serious tsunami in the region was in 1889, thanks to folklore, they knew that as the ocean suddenly began to recede, a more than equal and opposite reaction was imminent. As for the animals, they either pre-empted the knowledge or confirmed what was about to transpire. Either way, these primal people paid attention to what was happening around them.

While it is sad, it should not be surprising to learn of the significant death toll on the islands of Nicobar, immediately south of the Andamans. These islands are tourist oriented. The shoreline animals and the traditional stories have been replaced by modern buildings, modern technology and the news of the world. This is not the fault of technology, for modern technology is a significant part of the "field" of information. The December 26 tsunami was picked up by seismological instruments off the coast of Hawaii fifteen seconds after the earthquake occurred. As far as we are aware, this is faster than the known capabilities of any animal. The problem was, no one knew quite what to do about it, who to warn or how to relay the message. Human technology has to be seen and understood in an evolutionary light – how is it being used, where is it taking us and at what cost to our relationship with our wild nature? The great Nature-poet, William Wordsworth answers this question in his poem, "The world is too much with us":

> The world is too much with us; late and soon,
> Getting and spending, we lay waste our powers:
> Little we see in Nature that is ours;

We have given our hearts away, a sordid boon!
This Sea that bares her bosom to the moon;
The winds that will be howling at all hours,
And are up-gathered now like sleeping flowers;
For this, for everything, we are out of tune;
It moves us not. – Great God! I'd rather be
A Pagan suckled in a creed outworn;
So might I, standing on this pleasant lea,
Have glimpses that would make me less forlorn;
Have sight of Proteus rising from the sea;
Or hear old Triton blow his wreathed horn.

What can we learn from these events at Yala and from the Andaman islands? Perhaps it is this: the animals are an extension of our eyes and ears and noses when we allow them to be. Weavers and herons know how high the rivers are going to rise when the rains come – the height of their nests above the impending water level will tell us. Hornbills regularly begin their nest building about ninety days before the first rains. The African titbabblers, mousebirds and crombecks, on the other hand, complete theirs about a month before the season of rain. Ants are ancient weathermen too. I have often seen them carrying their eggs to higher ground when the barometer begins to fall.

To be attuned to the natural world is not only to deepen one's awareness of the seasons and the rhythms of Nature, but to interpret and act upon the irregularities of Nature as well. It is to know that a midday howl of a hyena is never meaningless.

To rediscover ourselves in Nature, the idea of a mindfield is going to be an important one. And it is not new. To me, it is implicit in the "bushman" belief that all the animals say ONE thing. It is to see the Earth as does the British chemist James Lovelock in his *Gaia Hypothesis* (1972) as a living, self-regulating "superorganism" – a planet in touch with itself. From nitrogen-fixing to photosynthesis and the organic interplay of countless micro- and macro-organisms the idea of a super-organism is no mere metaphor. Far from being scientifically discredited, the idea has been a catalyst in bringing together the independent disciplines of microbiology, geography, geochemistry, evolutionary theory and astrophysics. To make the notion liveable, I want you to put on your poet's cap. I want you to "think molecular" or, to be more precise, to think in particles. I want you to be mindful of the continual exchange of atoms, particles and molecules around us. Everything in Nature is made up of atoms and particles including the human mind, for it too is a part of Nature.

It is impossible to speak about the mind without speaking about the brain, for it raises some testing neurological as well as philosophical questions, for example, are brains and minds the same thing? If the brain is confined to the skull, does that mean that the mind is confined there too? If it is, then human consciousness has to be understood as a purely intra-cranial affair, purely genetic and therefore capable of developing independently of our external and internal environments. If not, then our minds need to be understood as being both a product and a function of what is internal and external to us. But where do we draw the line between our inner and outer environments? Perhaps there is no line at all.

B eginning with a brief review of what some biologists believe are the evolutionary origins of the brain, let's examine some of the theories, evidence and implications for the brain–mind–environment continuum. In chapter two we acknowledged the evolutionary significance of symbiosis – the living together of two or more organisms for mutual benefit. One of the examples involved the symbiotic intrusion a little over a billion years ago of the highly mobile, corkscrew-like spirochetes into their new single-cell hosts. Today there are several evolutionary biologists who, like Lynn Margulis of the University of Massachusettes in Boston, regard these spirochetes as the precursors of the interconnecting pathways in our brain. How did this come about? It is believed that a number of these so-called "wrigglers", once inside the host cell, joined up end to end – an act of keeping in touch with each other. John Briggs and F David Peat write:

> Sacrificing their mobility, the spirochetes were trans-muted into brain cells where eventually, they became packed together, essentially immobile in our skulls. However, it would appear that their formal identity has been retained. These transmuted bacteria are today the instruments of the most rapid transit feedback network in the history of our planet. In what would seem a flicker of electrical motion, they no longer spin through primeval mud but through the furthest reaches of space and time – as the lightning fast mobility of human thought.

Genetically specified and regulated by the action of specific chemicals known as neurotransmitters, the "hard-wired" pathways in the central nervous systems of reptiles, birds and mammals are the ones that account for our basic emotional responses to the environment, our primary instincts or drives, our senses (sight, sound etc) and our motor functioning. Called the pathway or channel systems, it is well known that when an individual suffers a "stroke" in which such a pathway is involved, the result is a loss of function of the target muscles or organs involved.

On the other hand, our inner "state" – the way we feel, interpret, experience, reflect upon and modify our responses to the environment – appears not to be wired at all. Our inner state cannot be pinned down to any one or other pathway. Instead, in association with different neurotransmitters to those in the pathway or channel systems, the neurons responsible for our inner state act globally. In other words, the connections of these neurons interact and overlap with each other in what is aptly referred to as a "field of influence". This brings us back to the brain-mind conundrum.

Very basically, there are those who say that the brain and the mind are the same thing and those who say they are not. Both theories, as we shall see, are flawed by the same problem, namely, we know that our neurons are active while we are thinking, but neither theory is able to explain exactly how our thoughts cause our neurons to start firing and vice versa. Either way, we cannot escape the fact that our minds are a reality upon which our brains and our bodies depend and that we are a mindful species, for as Solms and Turnbull remind us, our minds are "... the part of nature that we ourselves occupy. It is us."

The dualists, with whom the philosopher Descartes (1596–1650) is associated, believe in the dichotomy of mind and matter, body and soul and in this case, brain and mind. To them, the brain and the mind are not the same thing. They believe that mental and neural processes may interact or even co-occur (Descartes thought that the pineal gland was the point of interaction) but they are ultimately irreducible to one another. In other words, the mind has no substance or physical properties. It exists as a kind of ghost in the machine.

A classic example of dualist thinking is intrinsic to the notion that psychiatric conditions such as irritable bowels and bladders, phobias, obsessions, compulsions, panic episodes, anxiety neuroses and depression, are, because they cannot be measured, "all in the mind". In other words, the physical condition does not exist. Acknowledging that mental processes have an influence on bodily processes, they nevertheless maintain that the mind is an autonomous entity and that in certain conditions, all that is needed is that the patient get his or her mind "right".

The monists on the other hand, with whom the Dutch philosopher, Spinoza (1632–1677) is most closely associated, believe that the physical and mental are aspects of the same reality organised in different ways. In the way that the brain can be understood to be a function of the body, they see the mind as a second-order function of the brain. In other words, in the way that a magnetic field emerges from electric currents in a coil of wire, mind emerges from neural activity in the form of mental fields. "Mental" or "psychiatric" conditions are therefore not in the mind, they are in the "body-mind". When viewed in an evolutionary light, this connection is significant, the reason being that many of the above-mentioned psychiatric conditions, because of their link to survival-oriented emotion pathways, may, at some level, have been appropriate or even adaptive. The roots of these conditions are therefore not necessarily pathological. Because of this it is important to point out the potential survival function of these conditions (even though they have become maladaptive). This approach goes a long way towards relieving these patients of a sense of guilt and hopelessness about themselves.

While my leanings are very much towards the monist school, I am nevertheless not entirely convinced by the reductive argument – the mind being ultimately reducible to the properties of neurons (nerve cells). As important as the neurons are, to pin the mind to our neurons will inevitably take us to the level of the genes and to the premise that our brains and our minds are purely genetic in their origin. I appreciate the significance of the genetic "push", but, in the same way that electrons are "pulled" into an electromagnetic field, what about the "pull" of the environment in the shaping of our bodies, brains and minds?

One of the best examples I know confirming the notion of the environmental "pull" involves the natural history of stem cells. Stem cells are the non-specific, embryonic precursors or "ancestors" of every functional cell in our body. What happens to them – their functional destiny – depends on the physiological environment into which they are "pushed" or "pulled". In other words, for a stem cell to become a brain cell, it has to be nurtured within a brain cell environment. The genetic predisposition (the "push") to become a brain cell is simply not enough. It also needs a "pull". The same goes for liver cells, heart cells, muscle cells and so on. At this stage, the process of stem cell differentiation is not entirely understood, but the medical implications are profound. By infusing stem cells into "irreparably" damaged tissue, new growth of healthy cells can, in theory, be initiated.

It would appear, then, that the brain–mind relationship is not only genetically primed, but environmentally nurtured as well, or, as Spinoza poetically put it: "mind and matter are a double aspect of a single substance".

THE ENVIRONMENT AND THE STRUCTURING
OF OUR BRAINS

Two academics offer a compelling theory for the role of the environment in the ultimate structuring of our brains. They are Professor Judith Toronchuk of the Department of Psychology and Biology at Trinity Western University in British Columbia and George Ellis, professor of Mathematics at the University of Cape Town who won the prestigious Templeton Award in 2004 for his contributions to science and religion. To me, their thinking is a significant step toward the conventional support for a continuum of the waves, particles and molecules of mind and matter. But first, some important biological background.

Every human being is made up of at least ten trillion cells – more than the total number of stars in any known galaxy. The vast majority of these cells are neurons and their neuronal connections, a powerful reminder that we are a thinking, feeling and sensory species. Every cell in our bodies has a nucleus. In each nucleus there are forty-six paired chromosomes (twenty-three from your father and twenty-three from your mother). Each chromosome is made up of packed helical strands of DNA, the carriers of our genes.

There are roughly twenty-five thousand genes in every human cell. These genes are what we refer to as the human genome – the blueprint of the human animal. And as we now know, mammals of all species share more than ninety percent of our genome.

Ellis and Toronchuk believe that there are too few genes in the human genome to account for the disproportionately large number of nerve *connections* in our bodies. There are at least ten billion such connections. They write:

> Remembering that the information in the human genome
> has to cover the development of all other bodily structures
> as well as the brain, this is not a fraction of the information

required to structure in detail any significant brain modules, let alone for the structuring of the brain as a whole.

Put simply, on the available information about how neuronal connections are established, it would appear that there are too few genes to account for the variety and complexity of these connections. What else then, other than our genes, could be the stimulus for the detailed structure of the neural connections? "Our environment," they say. The question, of course, is not only how, but why?

Staying with Darwin's principle of natural selection – organisms with characteristics that best fit them for survival are the ones that contribute most offspring to the next generation – they combine the ideas of the neurobiologists Gerald Edelman and Jaak Panskepp to explain the brain-environment link. According to Edelman, our neurons with their connections are the structures that have best adapted to our environment and therefore they are the ones that account for the most numbers. This may sound rather simplistic but remember, every functioning cell was at some stage in its early evolution an individual organism which, over millions of years of adaptation, became the cells that form the tissues, organs and systems in the different plant and animal species on Earth today. The rules of natural selection apply not only to different species but to simple cells and their connections as well. In other words, without a dynamic environment there would be very little to adapt to and hence little need for the existing number, variety and complexity of neural connections. To me, this goes a long way towards explaining the "why" of the brain-environment link.

What about the "how"? This is where the invitation to think molecular or "particular" could help us. Think about it: every perception of an outside event – hearing, seeing, smelling, tasting and touching – is essentially the result of a disturbance in the particle field around us. Within the narrow parameters of human perception, we are not only sensitive to this disturbance but we are able to interpret and localize the source of it as well. In other words, in the same way that we consciously and unconsciously interpret the information given by our neuro-chemical systems and pathways, we also interpret the information transmitted along what could be described as particle "pathways" in the external environment. But there is more. Our perceptions, both internal and external, are always emotionally charged. Every interpretation of what is going on around us or within us, is accompanied by a *feeling*. Our outer environment, therefore, is never merely a geographical setting. From positive to negative, every environmental encounter evokes a particular feeling – pleasure, awe, fascination, disappointment, sadness, fear, panic, disgust, anger, indifference etc.

Drawing on Jaak Panskepp's descriptions of the "hard wired" primary emotion-command pathways in mammalian brains, Ellis and Toronchuk suggest that the large number of neural connections over and above those that are genetically primed, are determined by our ongoing emotional responses to our inner and outer environments. Communicated via external, particle pathways of light, sound, smell and touch to the internal emotion pathways and centres of our brains, the outer environment, because it is a constant source of subjective, survival-oriented information, shapes our immune and endocrine systems. It is a "switchboard" of emotional triggers that sculpt and mould not only our behaviour but the structure and function of our brains as well. Looked at in this light, our entire existence is dependent on this interaction with the environment. Our minds therefore exist to make sense not only of the neurochemical information of our bodies, but as a precondition for regulating and making sense of the waves and particles that connect us to the objects and events in the world around us. Poetically, if the eye looks, then the mind "sees". If the ear hears, the mind "listens". And it does so *feelingly*. Through mind, we can conjure an image of ourselves, we can turn objects into symbols and a life into a narrative. The mind, which includes a tiny, conscious portion known as the ego, has evolved not only to reach out into the world but to be receptive to that which is reaching for us.

The notion of a mindfield as an interplay of ideas, dreams, intentions and like-mindedness is an echo of what the archaeologist and excommunicated Jesuit, Teilhard de Chardin, courageously referred to as the noosphere in his 1959 book, titled *The Phenomenon of Man*. The noosphere is a "thinking layer" or a "field" of thought. He imagined it as a layer over and above the biosphere, emerging from the first moment that a living creature became aware that it was aware. It was a quantum leap of consciousness. Suddenly, there existed on Earth a creature who understood the concept of time, mortality, individuality, relationship and belonging. According to Teilhard, from that moment, near the end of the Tertiary period – only a million and a half years ago - the world took a giant evolutionary step forward. Rilke would have said, it took a step "out of its house". From that moment, the world began to enter a new age. Better still, says Teilhard, it began to find its soul.

If that first acknowledgement of kinship, belonging and home was the first conscious act of soul, then to me, that first act of reaching out into a world beyond oneself, to an invisible world of possibilities and interlocking forces, was the first spiritual act. It was the beginning of a new-found awareness which, like the biological matrix from which it had evolved and from which it was imminent, sought to continue itself. The relationship between subject and object would change forever. It was the beginning of a "field" in which a collective consciousness would become increasingly prominent. Human thoughts, ideas and intentions had not only taken wing, but they were destined to interact also. Poetically, the human animal had extended a long arm into the world.

In a brilliant piece of analysis Karl Popper, in his account of the evolution of life, of man and of civilisations, took a closer look at the interplay between subject and object. He proposed that we live in an objective world of material things such as sticks, stones, brains and so on, and a subjective world of minds – an inner world of thoughts, feelings and interpretations of the objective world. He then proposed a further world consisting of objective products of the mind, all of which shape or influence the existence of the living creature. Examples of this in the animal world, writes Bryan Magee, "are nests built by birds, honeycombs, spider webs etc. all of these structures existing outside the body of the creature and which function to help the organism to solve its problems". Some of these "structures" are abstract, such as the social organisation of termites or the patterns of communication in different species.

The evolutionary significance of tangible and abstract creations in the human world, particularly those that are associated with the transformation of the physical environment (the wheel, modern technology and medicines to name a few) is that they then acquire central importance in the environment to which we then have to adapt ourselves. In other words, we are drawn to and influenced by our creations. They become part of the field of influence. Such creations, said Popper, include abstract creations like language, ethics, law, philosophy, religion, the sciences, the arts and institutions. Once "out there", he wrote, "these structures, in the human world at least, can be examined, evaluated, criticised, revised and when wholly unexpected discoveries are made within them, revolutionised." It is a world that refers to our entire intellectual heritage, including our cultural heritage, and, as Magee writes, "it is through our interaction with this world that we become selves," or, if you like, we become truly human. Our "creatureliness" manifests itself. How else could this reflective interplay occur if not via the same field or particle pathways that inform us about everything in our environment?

Common to both Teilhard and Popper, as I see it, is the notion that the human psyche exists not only "in here", so to speak, but "out there" as well. The psychological significance of this notion is profound. Unconfined to our skulls and to what is immediate, our geographical and cultural environment has become a dynamic extension of the psyche into which we project our autobiographical and collective selves. The world, in the process of human evolution, has become less of a stage and more of a mirror. It is an extension of a deep sense of belonging, for we identify with all manner of worldly creations, from animals and trees to people and places. And lest we forget, because we often don't

like what we see in ourselves, the world is also the target of our negative projections.

FIELDS OF INFLUENCE

What follows are propositions from philosopher-scientists that deserve attention for one reason more than any other – they are exploring ideas that could transform the way we think about learning, intelligence and consciousness. In their own way, they are exploring the notion of a mindfield. What is clear is that these theorists have a great love and respect for science.

The first of these theorists is the botanist and author Rupert Sheldrake. Sheldrake has been interested in "field" theories for a long time. At Cambridge University in the 1980s, while doing research on the development of plants, he revisited the age-old question of how plants grow from simple embryos into the characteristic form of their species. How do the leaves of willows, palms and roses take up their shapes, he asked? These were questions concerning the subject of morphogenesis, the coming into being of form (from the Greek *morph*, or form, and *genesis*, or coming into being) – apparently one of the great, unsolved mysteries of biology.

In the same way that Ellis and Toronchuk question the emphasis on the genetic influence in favour of environmental triggers in structuring our brains, Sheldrake too believes that it is too simplistic to attribute morphogenesis to mere genetic programming. He believes in specific, non-genetic, "morphic fields" that include social and cultural fields, molecular, behavioural and mental fields and he thinks they all have one thing in common: they contribute towards the organization of the systems within that particular field. A good example of this is the amazing way that flocks of birds fly at high speeds without colliding with each other. Another example is the way that shoals of fish, when threatened, like a single organism suddenly change direction, scatter and then reform. The dilemma is obvious. Is it sufficient to say that the

genetic neurophysiology of birds and fish are such that they can select-
ively avoid mid-flight or mid-swim contact or do they fly or shoal within a "field" of information and influence that shapes and patterns their
flight or swim? Perhaps it is both.

Sheldrake is well aware of the scepticism he has evoked. He acknowledges that he does not know the origins of morphic fields or of how
they evolve, but through well-documented experiments on termite
"communication", pets who "know" when their owners are coming
home and the human sense of being stared at (see mirror neurons in
chapter eight), he nevertheless believes these fields exist. They may be
there as a matter of pure chance, or perhaps as a result of some inherent creativity in mind and Nature, he says, but they exist and, in true
evolutionary style, they bring with them a kind of memory, a signature
or a pattern of what has gone before. What is more, he writes, "once a
new field or pattern of organization comes into being, then through
repetition, this field becomes stronger. The same pattern becomes more
likely again." In the human realm, says Sheldrake, "this kind of collective memory is closely related to what C G Jung called the collective
unconscious".

Providing a scientific way of thinking about ends, purposes goals and
intentions, the mathematician René Thom, in a branch of mathematics
called Dynamics, has constructed mathematical models that support
Sheldrake's field theory. These models focus on what Thom calls
"attractors" – a field of influence towards which biological systems are
pulled or developed. Imagine an eddy spinning in a flowing river. Now
imagine a group of eddies, some of them moving closely together others
coalescing. This image is a metaphor for the way "attractors" work. As in
the notion of a mindfield, they are in the same river, the same process,
they develop, they become different expressions of the same substance,
they have a life and a death, they have influence and are in turn influenced by each other and by their surroundings. Is it too poetic to imagine that we live in a field in which eddies of like-mindedness are not
only drawn to each other, but merge according to the intensity of the
attraction? And what about an eddy as an individual life, eventually,

upon death, returning to the substance from which it was formed? Or the realisation that it is the substance (Nature) that is eternal and not the autobiographical self?

Another view of a "mindfield" is that of the scientist Richard Dawkins, author of *The Selfish Gene*. He considers the possibility that we have given birth to a new and more rapid kind of evolution involving culture rather than chemicals. Genetics has genes, so culture, he believes, must have its own units of transmission. He calls these cultural units *memes*. Memes, he says, are thought processes – ideas, notions, images, fantasies, symbols, tunes, fashions, methodologies, strategies, philosophies that become part of a "meme-pool", infiltrating the thought processes of individuals who are either sensitive to, or ready for them. They can be understood as projections of consciousness striving to continue their existence in a new creature. In Dawkins' words "they leap from brain to brain" or, as Sheldrake suggests, they are passed on not only from ancestors to their descendants, but move sideways from one group of organisms to another across gaps of space and time.

Lyall Watson, drawing on the principles of natural selection, sees memes as living structures capable of implanting themselves in another mind like viruses which parasitize the genetic mechanism of a host cell. He adds that they are then forced, as viruses are, to compete with one another in a truly Darwinian fashion. In other words, they compete for access to minds that will ensure their survival.

If natural selection does operate at the level of thought processes, then it is clear that fashions and philosophies, particularly those that come and go, are good examples of evolutionary cul-de-sacs. In a sense, we are porous to thought processes that are both conscious and unconscious and the memes that survive and which are successful are the ones that are in the right place at the right time – the ones that fulfil our immediate as well as our long-term needs. They stand the test of time.

THE BRAIN-ENVIRONMENT INTERPLAY

Deep in the left and right temporal lobes of our brains is a constellation or nucleus of highly sensitive nerve cells known as the amygdala, the Latin name for almond – a description of the shape of this constellation of cells. Thanks to the work of the neurobiologist Paul Whalen and his colleagues, we now know that the amygdalae are able to detect emotionally-charged situations, even if we are not aware that we are in that situation. What is more, if the situation or activity is one of fear or anger, the right-side amygdala is particularly active. The sensitivity of these nuclei then, do not depend on selective attention to what is going on. Could this unconscious sensitivity to what is happening around us be the basis for what we often refer to as intuition or the gut-feel? To me, the following clinical findings point in this direction:

In medical terminology, there is a condition known as "functional" blindness. In these patients, the eyes as well as the optic pathways are intact. They are blind as a result of damage to the occipital region of the brain – the area responsible for the reception and interpretation of visual images. Although blind, these patients nevertheless "pick up" on the ambience or emotional state of their immediate surroundings. In these patients, not only do the amygdalae remain sensitive to emotion-charged images and situations, but so does another region – situated low and towards the middle of the frontal lobe – the ventro-medial prefrontal cortex. Unlike the amygdalae, this area appears to be crucial for discerning the emotional *significance* of the prevailing stimulus or situation – clearly, a more complex form of discernment. This is the key brain-region for experiencing empathy, sympathy and compassion, i.e. the sharing of feelings: the pain, the joy and the circumstance of another. So, this is where our evolutionary antennae are hidden.

What is really important in these clinical findings is, as the neurologist Antonio Damasio puts it, "the barrier of blindness has been broken through". In other words, in terms of our survival and of the power of the all-seeing eye, the retina is a secondary, more recent phenomenon than our internal antennae. Seeing, on its own, is not the precondition for believing. Feeling is.

But what about long-distance interactions? How can one explain the following story, told to me by one of my patients, a young woman in her mid-twenties? Which parts of her brain were active in the unfolding of these events? The year before coming to see me she was living in England, thousands of kilometres from her home in South Africa. She began to experience frontal headaches and with them, an increasing fear that her father was suffering from a malignant brain tumour. Repeated telephone calls to her home were met with the assurance that her father was in good health. Several weeks after the onset of the headaches and while her fears for her father were still present, her mother phoned her in London to tell her that her father was to undergo emergency surgery for a brain tumour. "My mother's words, when she phoned to tell me" she said, "could have been mine".

What was I to say, for I was well aware that an important part of this young woman's grieving process was to come to terms not only with her premonition, but with a deep-seated guilt that her father's death may have had something to do with her own thought processes. "Every time I had these thoughts about him, I had to keep pushing them away. I didn't want to tempt fate," she said. But fate had already dealt its hand. The tumour, albeit asymptomatic, was already established when it was "picked up" by the daughter all those weeks before the diagnosis was made. Pablo Neruda touches on this mystery in the lines of his poem, "And I Watch my Words":

> And I watch my words from a long way off.
> They are more yours than mine.
> They climb on my old suffering like ivy.

From children to adults, we all have death thoughts about siblings, spouses and parents for which we often feel guilty and we all, even the most hardened of us, have those uneasy moments when we believe that we are tempting fate. I don't think that we need too much convincing to acknowledge that old biblical admonition that what we fear will come upon us. As irrational as it may seem, it is as if our negative thoughts and fears magnetize the "field" around us. But it works the other way too. We can put positive thoughts, images and feelings into the field as well. What happens to these products of the mind? If the brain, the mind and the environment are a continuum then the logical answer is that they become part of an extended field of influence. Is it too much to imagine that they enter the mindfield where they are then picked up or rejected by other minds? Do we not attract like-mindedness?

An excellent example of an extended field of influence comes from the astonishing observations of macaque monkeys by Japanese scientists in the 1950s. What they observed was equivalent, in monkey terms, to the harnessing of fire. A young female macaque, a resident on one of a group of islands, was seen taking soil-covered plant bulbs to nearby seawater pools to clean them before eating them. As the human observers watched, this idea took root and spread, slowly at first but with gathering momentum until it became general practice not only throughout the entire island colony, but on the surrounding islands as well. Lyall Watson calls this the "hundredth monkey phenomenon" meaning that it takes only a certain number of like-minded individuals to create an idea or an image that will find its way through the world.

Finally, can we share the "field" of another species? The answer to this question might not be that far off and the animal that could show us the way is our traditional best friend – the dog. In his research on epileptic patients who own dogs, Stephen Brown, a British neuropsychiatrist and specialist in epilepsy has found that a significant percentage of the dogs in his study were able to detect an impending seizure in their owners anything between fifteen and forty-five minutes prior to the event. To communicate the impending event, the dogs would approach the owner and begin pawing or barking, or both. Another of his findings is that no particular breed is found to be better at sensing an oncoming seizure than any other. In all cases, however, probably because the dog owners were able to prepare themselves, the frequency of seizures were reduced. In fact, many were able to abort the event altogether.

Considering the quality of life of patients suffering from epilepsy, these findings are hugely significant. The important question of course is – how do they do it? Do they pick up cues from their human companions such as a change in body language, mood or behaviour? So far, we don't know. What we know, however, is that patients suffering from temporal lobe epilepsy often experience what is medically referred to as an aura. This is a peculiar sensation or phenomenon that precedes and marks the onset of the seizure. For some, the aura could be one of entering a dream-like state or of becoming disoriented. Others may experience alterations in their sense of taste, hearing or body movements. Then there are those patients who don't experience an aura at all and yet the dogs still respond to the impending event. Clearly, the electro-chemical event preceding a seizure is not restricted to the brain but extends beyond it into a "field" to which our canine companions are sensitive.

In his fascinating book *Dogs Who Know When Their Masters Are Coming Home*, Sheldrake has convincingly shown that certain dogs, through distinctive and timely changes in their behaviour and over considerable distances (fifteen to twenty-five kilometres away) become instantly aware of the home-coming intentions of their owners. How else could this be possible if not through a "field" which at present we may suspect, but which we know little about? And what intentions do we unwittingly communicate to animals, to plants and to our human companions? I will address this question in chapter eight.

QUANTUM FIELDS

Modern physics reminds us that the interaction and influence of particles occurs in a quantum field that exists throughout space and where the speed or the timing of the influence of particles, one upon another, is instantaneous. According to Einstein's 1905 special theory of relativity, the notion of separate particles having an instantaneous influence on each other was inconceivable. Also known as the "law of local causes", this theory proposed that events in the universe happened at speeds that did not exceed the speed of light. However, after some exquisite mathematical reasoning, Einstein eventually challenged his own theory and in 1935 he and his colleagues came up with a new proposal: "the change in the spin of one particle in a two-particle system would affect its twin *simultaneously*". Absurd? No. In 1964 the physicist John S Bell proposed that there is an elemental oneness to the universe, a proposal that would become known as Bell's theorem. He theorised that particles operate and influence each other within a "field". His theory put a restraint on the belief that the influence of particles, one upon the other, is limited to the speed of light. But how could it be proved? In 1972, in an experiment involving photons, calcite crystals and photomultiplier tubes, John Clauser of Berkeley University validated Bell's theory. It was true – the quantum field was for real. Particles, over distances, do influence each other instantaneously, a validation of the astrophysicist Arthur Eddington's quip "when the electron vibrates, the universe shakes." And what about that ancient poetic notion, "pick a flower, disturb a star?"

In his delightful book, *The Tao Of Physics*, Fritjof Capra describes this field as "a continuous medium that is present everywhere in space." He adds that "particles are merely condensations of the field; concentrations which come and go, thereby losing their individual character and dissolving into the underlying field." We are living in a mindfield and if this sounds ecological, then say yes, quickly.

SYNCHRONICITY

If thoughts, secrets, intuitions and intent are indeed mobile, then synchronicity, the so-called meaningful coincidences in our lives, will begin to make sense. Synchronicity describes events that do not appear to have any causal link, but because of the so-called coincidences of these events, they are linked, instead, by meaning. We all have experiences of such coincidences: we may be thinking of someone we haven't heard from for a while and then the telephone rings. We pick it up to hear that person's voice on the line. Or perhaps, somewhere in the wild, while thinking about a particular elephant it suddenly appears from out of a thicket. We sometimes need a particular item, wondering where or how we might find it and then, inexplicably, it presents itself – exactly what was needed. We all have stories, incidents and "co-incidents" when we say we just happened to have been in the right place at the right time. It is as if, however briefly, there is a palpable meeting between psyche and substance. The feeling is one of being immersed in a field of actions, interactions and feedback. It is as if we have touched a potential that has been lost and if not, a gift of Nature that we are beginning to unwrap. It is an implacable sensing that everything in the universe is connected.

To illustrate what could be a link between the mobility of ideas and synchronicity, the analytical psychologist Marie-Louis von Franz, in her essay "Science and the Unconscious", draws attention to Darwin and his theory of the origin of the species:

> Darwin had developed his theory in a lengthy essay, and in 1844 was busy expanding this into a major treatise when he received a manuscript from a young biologist unknown to him. The man was A R Wallace whose manuscript was a shorter but otherwise parallel exposition of Darwin's theory. At the time, Wallace was in the Molucca Islands of the Malay Archipelago. He knew of Darwin as a naturalist, but had not the slightest idea of the kind of theoretical work on which Darwin was at the time engaged. In each case, a creative scientist had independently arrived at a hypothesis that was to change the entire development of biological science. Backed up later by documentary evidence, each had initially conceived of the hypothesis in an intuitive "flash".

The logic of cause-and-effect-thinking tells us that synchronicity is statistically improbable and yet it happens time and again. What is striking is the way it promotes a sense of continuity, how it narrows the gap between our inner and our outer lives and how it links subject and object. It can't be pinned down or called upon at will, a reminder that it is not an ego-skill such as memory or intellect, something to be measured or worked at. Rather, it is mercurial, experienced as something that happens to us unexpectedly, dramatically and, sometimes, poetically.

But why should we be interested in this? Well, if we are interested in the human factor in Nature, then we need to be interested in everyday life and everyday people also. Meaning and the quest for it, as suggested, is a defining characteristic of the human animal. It is central to the goal of psychotherapy also – the task of trying to derive and to establish meaning out of our situations, our personal suffering and our discontent.

In addition to living in a world of cause and effect, ours, by virtue of the importance of meaning, is also a world of correlation and affect. This is to say that the logical connections we make about our world are often incomplete until there has been an emotional connection as well. We are born patternmakers, linking the whirling patterns of fingerprints to the spiralling shapes of galaxies, and we do it because it *feels* right. We find elephant footprints and other animal images in cloud patterns and we are all "experts" at reading the signs of the times. We are superstitious even when we try not to be. Predictability and control are either sides of the same coin. We say things come in threes, what goes around, comes around and we warm to the alchemical admonition: as above, so below.

As irrational as it may seem, symbol formation and pattern making are part of our survival. We can't help it. If we can't find the connecting patterns, we tend to create them and it does not matter that they do not obey the laws of cause and effect. We correlate because it is intrinsic to our search for meaning. "Whatever else the unconscious may be," said Jung, "it is a natural phenomena which produces symbols and these symbols prove to be meaningful." And then there is synchronicity – that occasional yet deep sense of being part of a field of meaning. What follows is a true story.

A friend of mine, a retired architect and long distance runner, began feeling tired and short of breath during a sequence of early morning runs. At first he ignored the symptoms, putting them down to the summer heat and a lack of physical fitness. At the same time, the pump at the borehole on his property began to malfunction. Upon closer examination, he concluded that the water pipes leading from the pump had become corroded and clogged, increasing the pumping pressure on the machine. Instead of replacing the pipes, he made intermittent attempts to unclog them providing temporary benefit to the pump and to the flow of water into a reservoir near the homestead.

He then began to notice that each time he went down to investigate the borehole, he would experience the strange shortness of breath that he had experienced while running. Two seemingly unconnected actions followed. Firstly, he had the pipes replaced with new ones and secondly, he consulted his doctor about his symptoms. The visit to his doctor resulted in triple by-pass surgery for advanced occlusion of his major coronary arteries. Upon returning home from the hospital, he took a walk through his garden. What he saw – the strong clear flow of water pumping out of the bore-hole into the reservoir – had a huge impact on him. In an instant, this highly educated, mechanically minded man ventured into the realms of the absurd – he linked the blocked pipes of the water system with his "blocked" arteries. "Were the clogged pipes a reflection or a forewarning of his own cardiovascular condition?" he asked of himself. I don't have to tell you the answer to his question other than to say that for him, correlating the two seemingly separate events was inescapable, or at least necessary. It is likely that we would have done the same.

Another facet to this story, seen from a depth psychology perspective, addresses the difference between healing and fixing. This man, by virtue of the cause and effect nature of the surgical procedure, had every reason to regard himself as fixed. His sense of healing, on the other hand, came through the powerful synchronistic correlation between the conditions at the bore-hole and his own cardiovascular condition. To try and convince this rational man otherwise would be to waste one's breath. Neither you, nor I, could have stopped him from adding depth to what was superficially an irrational association. He knows about irrationality but he will never forget the profound sense of connection and meaning he gained from that man-machine interaction. It was as if they had spoken to each other. Sometimes irrationality has its own rationale.

A word of caution: I think we need to be careful of confusing synchronicity with the notion that every life incident is meant to be. Certain life events do not appear to have any meaning at all and it is up to us to decide whether or not to give them meaning. In other words, I disagree with those who support a predeterministic view that everything, from life threatening illnesses to personal and collective tragedies are meant to be. How can we possibly believe that tidal waves, earthquakes, human poverty, starvation, AIDS and man-made ecological crises are meant to be? We either give these tragedies meaning or not and, with time, we usually do. Sometimes it is precisely what happens after the second act – the act of giving meaning to an event - that determines one's openness to the events that are bound to follow. "Nothing has changed," says the unknown poet, "except my attitude – so everything has changed." On the other hand, even the sceptics among us, when we are honest, will admit that there have been certain events in our lives when the sense of meaning has been immediate and profound. There was no need for the second act. This is synchronicity.

To understand the deeper significance of synchronicity I believe it is important that we remain open to the likelihood that it works both ways. Events not only happen to us – we also happen to them. In other words, I think we need to become more aware of our personal contributions and influence (conscious or unconscious) to events that we tend to describe as synchronistic. Gary Zukav, in describing the "observer effect" in physics, offers a quantum perspective: "since particle-like behaviour and wave-like behaviour are the only properties that we ascribe to light, and since these properties are now recognised to belong not to light itself, but to our *interaction* with light, it would appear that light has no properties independent of us!" The observer "happens" to light and vice versa.

Ancient wisdom reminds us that this kind of thinking is not new, for in its essence, it describes the traditional Nguni African notion of "Umuntu...Ubuntu" which means "because of you, I exist". To me, our humanity is not defined by human fellowship alone but includes a subtle yet essential dependency on animals and landscape as well. The web or the field of life is inclusive not only of our immediate surroundings, our geology and our biology, but of deep space and time also. Could synchronicity be another name for the "language" of this field? If it is then we have little choice but to see what we call mind, differently. It is to see it as existing not encased by a skull, but in an extended field for which we are, in our own way accountable. We are responsible therefore not only for what we take from it, but for what we put into it.

To take on this responsibility is to take the notion of a mindfield seriously. It is to add another dimension to what it means to think molecular – intention. A "bushman" hunter describing the feeling of oneness that he has with his prey prior to the hunt is describing not only his intent, but the significance of that intent also – because somehow, his prey knows about it. D H Lawrence agrees with this notion when he writes that the fox is "dead" long before the hunter has pulled the trigger of his gun. It is as if the animal knows when it is being hunted, or, as Barry Lopez describes the imminent death of a moose in an encounter with a wolf, "...it is engaged in a conversation of death. The moose, standing quite still, its eyes fixed on the grey hunter, knows what is going to happen next. It is an ancient contract."

The Kalahari "bushmen" understand this contract. To them there is no hunt unless it is filled with intention, continuity and connection. There is no hunt unless the prey and the prayer of the hunter become the same thing. Prayer can be seen as a poetic "chemistry" of intent, effective not so much in its calculating, acquisitive sense, but in a way that St Paul may have meant it in his letter to the Corinthians when he said we should "pray unceasingly". To me, to pray unceasingly is to be continually mindful of the patterns of connections between all things, vigilant to one's participation in a field of life. It is what Rumi meant when he said: "If you are not with us faithfully, then you are causing terrible damage, but if you are, then you are helping people you don't know and have never seen." The poet is asking us to hold the patterns of connection; to hold the chemistry. To pray unceasingly is to think molecular. It is to see the small things, including oneself, in the bigger picture. It means being able to look at a green leaf differently, to see the science and the poetry in it, to be aware that you and the leaf are linked. It is an invitation to experience the transformation process of photosynthesis at work – photons of light combining with molecules of carbon dioxide and water to provide not only the energy necessary for the growth and survival of the plant, but producing the life-giving molecules of oxygen that we breath in. It is to have a sense of privilege at being privy to the powerful yet delicate connection and interdependence between the chlorophyll molecules that produce oxygen and the haemoglobin molecules of red-blooded animals that bind it. It is to hold one's breath and then to give it back again in the realisation that the chlorophyll and haemoglobin molecules are almost identical. What makes them different is the presence of a single trace element in each molecule – magnesium in the former, giving plants their green colouring, and iron in the latter, the reason why blood is red.

Then there is that great and essential element – water. To think molecular is to see it differently and to salute it, for there is no other substance on Earth quite like it. It makes up more than eighty percent of our body mass – a reminder of our aquatic origins. Absurd? Not at all. Salute the salty signature of the sea in the intracellular compartments of our blood and that of the streams and the rivers in the extra-cellular flow. Feel the electricity of the bonding of those two hydrogen atoms and the one of oxygen that make up the molecules of water, each of them acting like a tiny magnet and when you have done that, imagine not only the delicacy, but the necessity of a molecular bond that lasts a crucial, one-billionth of a second before unbonding and then rebonding again – it is what gives water its wetness.

In his hard-hitting poem, "Elemental", D H Lawrence has no problem seeing water and fire differently. Here are some lines ...

I wish men would get back to their balance among the elements and be a bit more fiery, as incapable of telling lies as fire is.

I wish they would be true to their own variation, as water is, which goes through all the stages of steam and stream and ice without losing its head.

In summary, to acknowledge a mindfield is to be aware of the dance of atoms around us and within us and to have a sense of being in conversation with these invisible aspects of our existence. It is to give synchronicity a face that is both evolutionary and immediate. It is to wake up to the fact that we are creatures in a universe about which we know so little, that the vast fields of dark matter and dark energy are not "out there" in deep space, but that we are in it and of it and that each one of us can make a difference to the world in which we find ourselves. It is therefore, more than anything, an attitude: one that is open to choosing the hard path, the one that E O Wilson calls the path of "volitional evolution". This is the difficult path of those who have decided to do something about their heredity and their fate and who are committed to playing their part faithfully.

Our task is to rediscover ourselves in Nature and the only way to do this, I believe, is to make the mindfield liveable. Clearly, this is an individual choice. We either continue to believe that someone or something else will rescue us, show us the easy way, or even take the hard path on our behalf, or we choose the opposite – we take it upon ourselves. We take the hard path, each one of us, in our own way and we take it gladly. And where or when does that path begin? It begins exactly where we are right now, when we look up to see the world as a mirror; when we discover that our sense of freedom and authenticity is linked to the well being and authenticity of others – and that includes the animals, the trees and the land. It begins when we are open to synchronicity without pretending to control it. This is what living in a mindfield is about.

Finally, does all of this imply that an ecological intelligence and one's personal notions of God are mutually exclusive? If anything, surely, it is the opposite. To me, the creative forces of the universe are neither distant nor impersonal. Are we not, every one of us, living expressions of these forces? As Jacquetta Hawkes reminds us, we are hardly more cut off from Nature than is a naked flame from the surrounding exchange of gases and moisture that sustain it. It would appear that every living creature is united both inwardly and outwardly with the beginning of life.

However, let us not be victims of wishful thinking. Whilst it is impossible to participate in our own fate without a deep sense of awe and gratitude for the forces of creation and evolution, it is important that we accept the great indifference of Nature. It does not exist to punish or to bless us; it is neither cruel nor loving, but we, the human animal, can choose not to be indifferent. We can choose to reach out, to take care and to love.

PART TWO

LOOKING AHEAD

Tonight
I want you to feel the blurred edge
between good and bad,
to say no to the urge to look away
or to take sides...
but to give
with both eyes

I make no apology for a fascination with the soft edge of science. It is here, it seems, that we get fleeting glimpses of strange shadows just beneath the surface of current understanding.

Lyall Watson

7

THE BLIND SPOTS

THE NOTION OF AN ECOLOGICAL INTELLIGENCE, OF LIVING IN A MIND-field and of the need for a poetic language – all for the purpose of a deeper awareness of the multifaceted relationship between humans and Nature – may sound appealing and even logical, but it is going to require rhetoric as well as logic, and that is not an easy task. I use the word rhetoric in its classical oratory sense – the art of persuasive language, the art of influencing the one who hears. To some, the notion may be too far-fetched, not in keeping with conventional wisdom and, in all probability, too difficult to apply.

Don't be surprised if, in some instances, the resistance to what the poets have been trying to say is as dismissive as it was about Galileo's moons. Change is always unsettling and often threatening but we must not shy away from it. We must face up not only to the mounting environmental pressures of our time, but to the nagging internal pressures also – the ones that urge us to come to terms with the significance and responsibilities of what it means to be the human animal. Who knows, we might find unexpected patterns or directions within the very pressures we are trying to avoid. Consider the surprising truth about the short range, sub-nuclear forces of intergalactic space, for instance. These are not detectable until they are crushed together by huge stellar pressures. And yet, says Karl Popper, these are the very forces that are responsible for holding together all the more complex atoms of the universe. When looked at differently, our external and internal pressures, like those massive stellar forces, could be both appropriate and necessary – a reminder that there would be no evolution of size, shape or consciousness without them.

The environmental pressures of our time could be the very pressures behind a new evolutionary leap – not another expansion in brain size, but of a consciousness and an intelligence that can redefine our sense of history, our sense of Nature and our sense of co-existence. I believe the pressure is on and that it has to be taken personally. It is in the heated poetry of Antonio Machado: *"... what have you done with the garden?"* It is in the voice of the ecologically intelligent Rainer Maria Rilke: *"... tonight, I want you to take a step out of your house"*. It is in the challenge of Rumi who asks: *"... are you faithfully with us?"*

To be ecologically intelligent will demand nothing less than the courage of Oedipus. It is to discover that Sophocles' timeless myth is far less a story of incest than of our ultimate responsibility as human beings – to be accountable and conscious of our citizenship. Looking deeper into the myth is to discover that Oedipus, in addition to his self-imposed banishment from his kingdom for having unwittingly murdered his father and then having married his own mother, decreed that his own eyes be put out. A much-loved king, the people under his rule were horrified. "How were you to know?" they wept. His reply was, to the average mind, absurd. "I should have known," he said. "I have no excuse." Psychologically speaking, to blind oneself is to look inwards. It is to develop what we most lack in our dealings with the outer world – insight. And so, as we face the environmental crises of our day, do we have it in us to say: "We have no excuse?" Or will we turn our heads, pretending we just did not see?

To be ecologically intelligent is to be unafraid of stretching the measured horizons of rational thought. "Only those who risk going too far, know how far they can go," said the poet T S Eliot, but that does not mean divorcing ourselves from the core of reason. It takes a certain willingness to go to that horizon and to look straight into the things that at first we don't understand. But that is the demand of science, is it not? It is certainly the demand of the poets. True science is like true poetry. It suppresses nothing. It acknowledges that reason is a precious human asset, but it knows that our

Cartesian reasoning cannot adequately explain the real experiences in our lives, the real human-animal stories, the synchronicities, or reasons why we come to the rescue of endangered species and of those who suffer.

Ecological intelligence is heretical, and yes, it is critical of what might be called the cult of rationality, but it is not rejecting of it. It is an intelligence that recognises that every creature exists within and beyond itself, that an animal is never just that – an animal. A human being is never just that, either. Every species in its own way is poetic, every individual a unique interacting component in a complex field of life. And if there is anything absurd about this way of thinking, then it is time to risk that absurdity. It is time to take our souls to the horizon.

So far, I hope that the poetry in this book has taken us a little closer to that edge, or, as Seamus Heaney puts it, to a sensing of "something coming right, of something moving for us, a little ahead of us". I hope that we have come a little further than we had expected.

And so, if promoting an ecological intelligence demands that we take a peep through an alternative telescope, then let's do it. I hope you will discover that it has little to do with the existence of far off moons and extraterrestrial life. Rather, it focuses on the here and now. It is about becoming more aware of the miracle of biology, of knowing that within and beneath the skin of our hands is a "universe" of unconscious life and that every cell that makes up the you and the me has its own individual life. It is also about coming to know ourselves, warts and all, as two-million-year-old creatures of soul, spirit and Earth and of being prepared to be changed by that awareness.

SCIENCE AND SUBJECTIVITY

The first blind spot or resistance to the notion of an ecological intelligence is that it is subjective, anthropomorphic, and therefore unscientific. My response to such a perception is to quote from Robert Pirsig's 1974 classic on science and subjectivity, *Zen and the Art of*

Motorcycle Maintenance, "If subjectivity is eliminated as unimportant ... then the entire body of science must be eliminated with it."

Anthropomorphic thinking – the tendency to ascribe human attributes to beings or things that are not human – is irresistible. As Jung noted, we need no elaborate proof to show that children think in this way ... they animate their dolls and their toys and with imaginative children it is easy to see that they inhabit a world of marvel and magic. To put oneself in the "skin" of the other is therefore not a passive phenomenon. It is an act that takes us beyond ourselves, towards the experience of a sense of relatedness and relationship with the other.

A stick, for example is never just a stick. It is also a detachable extension of an arm, which can reach, probe, scratch and protect. It can become a weapon. It can be thrown, taking the energy of the human deltoids, the biceps and the fist, with it. It is something to lean on, in which case it becomes an additional leg imbued with "muscles" and "ligaments" to support the human weight. It is as if the trajectory of the stick, the spear and the arrow not only reflects the trajectory of human thought, but stimulates it. From sticks to space rockets, the anthropomorphic principle has been a major catalyst for the creative imagination of science.

Another sensitive but nevertheless classic example of anthropomorphic thinking is in the Genesis image of a Creator and that human beings are made in the likeness of that image. Whether this image is right or wrong is beside the point. What matters is that we create these images and we do it, it would seem, because our sense of meaning as a social and psychological species depends on it. Consciously or unconsciously, the tendency to connect, to make symbols, to invent analogies and to see the world as an extension of ourselves has been of enormous significance for the development of the human mind. It is central to our notions of continuity and belonging.

Empirical science insists on objectivity – detaching one's personal feelings and prejudices from the subject under observation. And yet quantum physics reminds us that the very act of observing the other, because it involves an exchange of influence, is intrinsically subjective. Any observation will arouse feelings. Subjectivity, the act of putting oneself in the skin of the other, is unavoidable. It is essential, not only to the methodology of tracking wild animals by the hunter-gatherers of the Kalahari, but also to the tracking of atomic particles.

In his book *The Art of Tracking*, subtitled The Origin Of Science, Louis Liebenberg suggests that anthropomorphic thinking may be the *result* of the creative scientific imagination. In other words, an imagination that observes, analyses, interprets and synthesises, pre-empts the capacity to understand and predict the thoughts and feelings of others. He adds that this kind of thinking arises from the need of the tracker to identify with the animal in order to predict its movements. The tracker must therefore be able to visualise or internalise what it would be like to be that animal in its particular environment, suggesting a sense of observer-animal-environment continuity. Prediction of an animal's movements would appear to be impossible unless one had learned how to ask the question: "How would I respond if I was that animal in this environment and in these circumstances?" In short, you would have to think like an eland, an elephant or a fish. You have to put yourself into their skin.

Liebenberg continues: "In the process of identification with the animal, the tracker superimposes his or her way of thinking onto that of the animal, thereby creating a model of animal behaviour in which the animal is understood to have certain human characteristics". To do this, the tracker would not only have to be highly familiar with the ways of the particular animal he was tracking, but in all likelihood, would adopt some of the characteristics of the animal as well.

In an outstanding documentary on the Kalahari "bushman" hunters by Craig and Damon Foster entitled *The Great Dance*, one of the hunters describes the process of putting oneself in the skin of the other:

"I, !Nqate, live in the Kalahari. I know all the waterholes and pans around here, the places where the animals come. When you track an animal, you must become the animal," he says. "You feel a tingling in your armpits when the animal is close. These are the things we know. When tracking is like dancing ... this is the Great Dance ... you are talking with God when you are doing these things."

From the Kalahari Desert to the laboratory of the nuclear physicist, says Liebenberg, it is well known and expected that the hunter/experimenter's preconceived image of the process under investigation will determine the outcome of the hunt/observations. When the scientist has such a clear visual image, wrote L E Walkup, the nature of the seeing or the sensing is described as though the scientist felt like the object being visualised. In thinking about a phenomenon they are interested in, some physicists, even in highly abstract theoretical physics, may more or less identify themselves with a nuclear particle and may even ask: "What would I do if I were that particle?" According to the physicist M Deutsch, writing in 1959, these preconceived images are symbolic, anthropomorphic representations of a basically intuitive or, for some, an inconceivable atomic process. They are also a reflection of the boldness of the imagination of the scientist.

Putting this into practice, try sitting at a water hole in the wild for a while, watching a herd of antelope coming down to drink. It takes ages. The animals move a few steps and then stop. Some of them look around, nostrils flared, ears pricked. They move forward again and then suddenly they freeze. As if by command they all look beyond the waterhole. Your eyes follow and there, exactly where they are looking, is a solitary lion dozing in the mottled shade of an acacia. You catch your breath. A flock of doves take off from the near edge of the water precipitating a startled retreat. The tension belongs to you. But the antelope are thirsty and the process starts all over again. It is hot. Thirst begins to outweigh the threat of danger. You reach for your water bottle. The lion lifts its head and then flops back into a one-eyed sleep. The antelopes bristle with tension and a muscle in your shoulder begins to ache. You want them to drink and yet your muscles are filled with the same antelope uncertainty. You are in their skin. Their thirst and their vigilance belongs to you. For a while you have become the animal that you have been watching.

As you stay with the situation – the antelope, the lion, the doves, the water hole, the heat of the day and the land, the more coherent the relationship between you and the activities of everything going on around you becomes. The longer you stay with it, the clearer it becomes that you are linked, and as the writer David Abram puts it, you stand "face to face with another intelligence, another centre of experience".

Sometimes to really be with the other we have to put the book away ... we have to keep our necks still ... we have to shut our eyes. Try entering into the flow of Rilke's ink as he writes this poem for the Gazelle, *Gazella dorcas*.

> Enchanted thing: how can two chosen words
> ever attain the harmony of pure rhyme
> that pulses through you as your body stirs?
> Out of your forehead branch and lyre climb,
>
> and all your features pass in simile through
> the songs of love whose words, as light as rose-
> petals, rest on the face of someone
> who has put his book away and shut his eyes:
>
> to see you: tensed as if each leg were a gun
> loaded with leaps, but not fired while your neck
> holds your head still, listening ...

To put one's self in the skin of the other is at the core of poetry. It is a prerequisite for a sense of coherence and meaning. One thing is certain – the human animal cannot avoid it, for, as Lyall Watson writes in his book *Dark Nature*, we are born animists "...happy to believe that everything we encounter is alive, just as we are, and that all objects are equally able to encounter us". Sometimes, the feeling that is born out of these encounters is deeply religious, connecting and sacred. And it begins to slip away as soon as we think we know it, as soon as it becomes familiar, as soon as we begin to take it for granted. It is as if, as soon as the poetry is lost, the connection vanishes.

The call of the wild, of kinship and companionship is in our blood. The very act of asking the questions about what that animal, that stranger or that object would do if I were it, or what I would do if it were me, enhances not only a sense of a shared identity, but also our capacities for empathy and compassion. Without these capacities, both of which imply a sense of shared co-existence and suffering, there would be no science and there would be no society.

Modern science, then, need not be cold and impersonal. Instead, there's good reason for it not to be. Einstein put it this way: "It would be possible to describe everything scientifically (ie. objectively), but it would make no sense; it would be without meaning, as if you described a Beethoven symphony as a variation of wave pressure." I believe that as we review the animal-human interface, the gap will begin to be bridged when we acknowledge, in the words of the wildlife biologist and writer Douglas Chadwick, that "...when scientists warn about the dangers of anthropomorphism, what they are really concerned about are the dangers of breaking through into new and uncertain ground ... that it amounts to the same old fear of upsetting established ways of looking at the world that has always stymied the practitioners of science". Yes, we will make mistakes when, based on our own feelings, we make claims about the feelings of animals. But let's not make the mistake of denying that their feelings could be remarkably similar to ours, or worse, that they don't have feelings at all. Anyone who owns a dog, who has spent time with elephants, chimpanzees, baboons, dolphins or killer whales, knows that these creatures express what we sometimes call the sophisticated emotions of delight, joy, disappointment, even embarrassment, and that they grieve. And when it comes to our relationship with wild animals, we quickly discover that there is a difference between habituation and trust. Why not say so? Whose permission are we waiting for to enter that "uncertain ground" where the voice of our wild relatives will be heard? How long is it going to take to acknowledge that there is indeed a menagerie within each of us ... a wolf, a hyena, a lion ... a wild man and a wild woman.

POETRY

It is likely that the next blind spot to what is being proposed will come from those who feel that poetry has nothing to do with them. Poetry, they will tell you, is for the poets and the physicists. "We have more pressing issues to deal with ... we are not interested in poetry and besides, we don't like poetry," they will say. Agree with them and then tell them, in these selected lines, what the poet Marianne Moore says about that ...

> I, too, dislike it: there are things that are
> important beyond all this fiddle.
> Reading it, however, with a perfect contempt for it,
> one discovers in it after all,
> a place for guidance ...

That, surely, is the whole point: we need guidance. Tell them that poetry redresses the balance of things. Quick to add weight to the lighter scale, it is the poet in us who knows when things are unbalanced. Tell them that poets are the best watchdogs of the wild.

Poetry is a mirror – it asks us to look at ourselves. Where are you in this powerful poem, "The Fable of the Mermaid and the Drunks", by Pablo Neruda?

> All these men were there inside
> when she entered, utterly naked.
> They had been drinking and began to spit at her.

165

Recently come from the river, she understood nothing.
She was a mermaid who had lost her way.
The taunts flowed over her glistening flesh.
Obscenities drenched her golden breasts.
A stranger to tears, she did not weep.
A stranger to clothes, she did not dress.
They pocked her with cigarette ends and with burnt corks,
and rolled on the tavern floor with laughter.
She did not speak, since speech was unknown to her.
Her eyes were the colour of faraway love,
her arms were matching topazes.
Her lips moved soundlessly in the coral light
and ultimately she left by that door.
Scarcely had she entered the river than she was cleansed,
gleaming once more like a white stone in the rain;
and without a backward look, she swam once more,
swam toward nothingness, swam to her dying.

I wonder if there is anyone who has not at some stage in their lives identified with that mermaid and perhaps, at another stage, with the drunks? The poem is a clear reminder that unfamiliar ideas are bound to be rejected, sometimes, brutally. It is also a reminder that you have to learn how to "dress", to learn the language of the corporate body, of conservation and management boardrooms, if you are to make the notion of an ecological intelligence understandable and workable. At the same time, it is crucial that you do not disparage those who hold a different view of Nature. Do not underestimate the intelligence of the other.

If you are interested in what is raw and genuine, then you are interested in poetry, says Marianne Moore. I agree with her but right now, wherever you are, I am interested in *your* poetry. I am interested in those first wild and awkward words that find their way through your pen or pencil onto that first page of your notebook. I want to know whether you can see the moon not only as a satellite of the Earth but as a daughter in a tidal dance around her mother, or perhaps a migrant with a scarred belly, and whether or not animals can find their way into your skin? Just write it down ...

> Tonight
> I want you to see the moon
> as a migrant,
> to say yes to those pathways of scars
> through which animals curve their way
> into your skin
> and to know that a hungry belly
> is a wild thing

I want to know what it is that dies in you and what it is that resurrects when an animal or a forest dies or vanishes, forever. Could you put this down on paper, please?

Poetry is about learning to look and to write with both eyes – the one that measures and the one that refuses to be measured. If you are doing formal research writing, make space in your reports to describe the feeling that might come over you when you enter a forest or when you engage with an animal. Yours might not be the first technical report that describes a loss of a sense of proportion when surrounded by a herd of elephants or a flock of carmine bee-eaters. You will not be the first to include poetry or to describe the sense of the sacred in a dissertation, but you will be the first to do it in your own unforgettable way. Better that you let the poetry write you. Let it take you to that edge, to where there are no subjects and objects and let it bring you back again. Look carefully at what you have written and afterwards, if you hear yourself saying, "Where the hell did that come from?" then it is likely that what you have written is poetry.

Poetry is disarming. It challenges the limits of objective reality. It goes straight for the heart. It speaks to a forgotten side of ourselves. It rages. It protects. It is noble. "It is a violence from within that protects us from a violence without," says the poet Wallace Stevens. It heals. "It speaks like the rain," said Karen Blixen. It is a "requiem for a broken world" – the title of this poem by Barbara Fairhead:

> This is a song
> of loss and betrayal,
> of broken things
> and endings.
> This is a song
> of ancestral memories
> of ancient covenants
> and forgetting.
>
> There is a rage in me,
> and a sorrow
> and a song of grief
> so deep and full,
> my soul suffers the singing.
>
> There is a wound in me
> that shall not heal
> the deep wound of the kingdom,
> the wound of your kind

There is a wound in me that shall not heal, says Fairhead. For her, it is not a wound that cannot heal. Instead, it is deliberately left open and raw in order that it may be felt and mourned for, first. Even the finest of poets knows that there are places into which words cannot reach, says Stephen Watson. And so to mourn, he says, is one of the most exacting forms of inner work that a human being can undertake, and to grieve is the prerequisite of all healing. It is what this book is ultimately about.

Poetry is a language of hope. It inspires. It heals. It belongs. It is a Wild Gift. It goes for the jugular, like this poem by Mary Oliver, who pointedly tells us what we need to do if we are to rediscover ourselves in Nature:

You do not have to be good.
You do not have to walk on your knees
For a hundred miles through the desert, repenting,

You only have to let the soft animal of your body
Love what it loves.

Whoever you are no matter how lonely,
The world offers itself to your imagination,
Calls to you like the wild geese,
Harsh and exciting, over and over again,
Announcing your place in the family of things.

RELIGION

For some, because of the usual religious connotations of words like spirit and soul, the notion of ecological intelligence is bound to be off-putting. My response to this blind spot would be to offer a line from the poet John Keats: "Call the world, if you please, the 'vale of soul making', then you will find out the use of the world."

Taken literally, the word religion comes from the Latin root derivative *ligare*, which means to bind or to connect. If an ecological intelligence promotes a sense of connection or relatedness to the other or if it sees the world as a vale of soul making, then the answer has to be yes – it is religious. I think we are all in some way "religious", for it would appear that we cannot survive without a sense of connection, be it to one single living thing, to something wild, to a landscape, a domestic animal, an invisible deity or to the memory of someone we once loved. What is more, that ancient sense of relatedness to the other has been with us for a long, long time, for as E O Wilson writes:

> ...people need a sacred narrative. They must have a sense
> of larger purpose, in one form or another, however intel-

lectualised. They will refuse to yield to the despair of animal mortality. They will find a way to keep the ancestral spirits alive. If the sacred narrative cannot be in the form of a religious cosmology, it will be taken from the material history of the universe and from the human species. That trend is in no way debasing. The true evolutionary epic, retold as poetry, is as intrinsically ennobling as any religious epic.

To me there is something both soulful and sacred in the knowledge that there is a wolf in me ... and a fox ...and a fish.

If a sense of the sacred is included in the definition of religion, then the answer again is yes – ecological intelligence is religious, for it looks for the sacred in things. A sense of the sacred is not some kind of sentimental whim and neither should it be seen as "a frivolous side issue next to the 'real' concerns of hard science and economics", says Herbert Schroeder. It is deeply historical, deeply psychological and deeply human.

It must be remembered that there are many people who do not associate themselves with any officially recognised religion but who nevertheless have a deep and genuine sense of the sacred in certain forests, in wilderness areas and in the powerful notion that some things are simply not for sale. It is therefore crucial that we understand that the threat to the existence of wild nature is also a threat to the central spiritual value of many people's lives and that it will be met with fear then anger and then defiance. We must be careful, says Yeats, in these poignant lines:

> I have spread my dreams under your feet;
> Tread softly, because you tread on my dreams.

On the other hand, ecological intelligence is not a religion. It is without dogma or prescription. It is a personal discovery that you and I are deeply rooted in the history of our planet and that we have a debt to repay for what we have done to it. It is to discover that we exist in a vast web of life and that every creature, in its own way, is a soul-maker. And it is not about being loveable. It is about being elemental, as D H Lawrence might have put it, true to one's own variations as water is. It is an attitude reflecting a commitment to a sense of authenticity, of learning to speak for one's self, of remembering your ancient name. In these lines from Stephen Watson's interpretation of the "bushman" poem "What is your Name", how would you answer the homesick Kalahari hunter?

> Your name, your real !Xam name,
> what is it? Call it for me,
> say it out loud for me
> that I may hear once more
> its sound – what it is like.
>
> Tell me, what is your name,
> your true !Xam name?
> Call it, say it for me.
> I long to hear it now,
> the sound that it will make.
> And do not tell me stories.
> Do not deceive me.
> Talk only our own !Xam
> that I can truly hear you,
> how you speak our only tongue.
>
> But you, a !Xam like us,
> you do not tell us plainly.
> The country that is yours –
> what is its name? I say again:
> tell me where you come from.

And so, what is your name? Where do you stand? Where is your voice?

THE MISINFORMED PUBLIC

Another blind spot to ecological intelligence reflects the belief that decisions pertaining to our natural resources have little or nothing to do with the public and that ecological decisions are best left in the hands of the "experts". I have already outlined the powerful subjective, archetypal responses that are sometimes evoked in a public that does not agree with what it regards as the sometimes high-handed decision and policiy-making not only in conservation biology, but in other fields such as politics and medical health. A doctor might be an expert with respect to the diagnosis and management of a particular pathology, but he should be careful never to underestimate the intelligence of his patients. Their scepticism, but more than that, their criticism, is good for us. We need more than their signatures to take them along what we deem to be the appropriate path or course of action – we need their participation.

Scientists appreciate how important it is to present their work to the public and this alone is good reason to listen to their protest. They are not all misinformed or ignorant. Linked to the powerful evolutionary dynamics of fair play, protest does not necessarily reflect or respond to classical reasoning and rational persuasion. But this does not make it wrong. If anything, because it is so often vindicated, it would appear to have its own rationale. We must welcome it. Protest is often the key to the unlocking of hidden agendas, a reminder that every policy is worth a review. It should also be a reminder that the first rule of scientific investigation is to ensure that one's mind is not clouded by prejudice – a necessary prerequisite for distinguishing non-science from nonsense.

In spite of its intentions and its successes, the hierarchy of advanced science carries an inevitable shadow of which we need to be aware. As Louis Liebenberg says, it comes in the form of authoritarian elitism, an attitude that distances people with less background knowledge from both the advances and the limitations of science. "What do they know?" is a classical shadow question. We should also be asking "What is it that we don't know?" As scientists, we need to be aware that our way of thinking is not the only school of thought and that in certain situations, even when we believe that we are right, it could be no more "right" than any other value-system.

I think we need to become a lot more egalitarian in our attitude to the public. Egalitarianism does not mean that all things and all people are equal either in strength, or knowledge, or in intellect. Instead, it is a belief in the high value of equality and of the desirability of removing inequalities. It is an attitude that is both purposeful and democratic, one that reaches out with the intention not only of bringing out the best in the other but of learning from that other. And that means learning from the layman, the children, the forests and the animals.

The writings of the Scottish psychiatrist R D Laing, for instance, are a profound reminder that our psychiatric descriptions of the behaviour of people occur in a behavioural field that includes the psychiatrist. "The behaviour of the patient," he writes, "is to some extent a function of the behaviour of the psychiatrist." Laing, in a way, was referring to the observer effect in quantum physics. He was therefore cautioning us to be careful of who or what we label as dumb, stupid or insane.

The dynamics of the doctor-patient relationship is not that different from any relationship, be it human-human, individual-public or human-animal. In other words, we have to understand the existential position of the other, where they're "coming from" and how they experience us. History has shown that there will always be missing information in our decision making and that "they", our psychiatric patients, the uninformed public or a herd of elephants can, when we are willing to listen, teach us a lot about themselves and about us – the so-called experts.

For the record, here is a statement from an "authority" on wild animal behaviour. It comes from a 1956 report by the then director of the Uganda National Parks, who, in a damning and subjective statement, unwittingly declared his lack of understanding of the African wild dog, *Lycaon pictus*.

> "Wild dogs hunt in packs," he wrote, "killing wantonly, far more than they need for food and by methods of utmost

cruelty. They do not kill quickly as the lion does but often start to devour the antelope which is his victim before its life is extinct. They do more damage than almost any other carnivore, for whenever they enter a particular stretch of country, the disturbance they cause is so great, that for the time being, all buck are driven out. A particularly unpleasant characteristic is that they will, without hesitation, turn upon any member of the pack that falls by the way through wound or sickness and show no reluctance to consume their own kind."

From what we know about wild dogs today, this statement is frighteningly subjective and misleading. They will certainly fight with dogs from another pack but they do not turn on and devour members of their own. Their manner of hunting is anything but cruel. It is quick and efficient. What is more, their prey is shared and the order of eating is determined by the age of the individual members of the pack – the yearlings go first, followed by the adults who, if there are cubs at the den, will regurgitate portions of meat for them upon their return. There is nothing unpleasant about wild dogs at all. Unrelated to wolves and domestic dogs in terms of evolutionary bloodlines, they serve as a model for the human animal when it comes to teamwork and care of the young. Sadly, they are highly sensitive to diseases such as canine distemper, and therefore, to the encroachment of human populations on their ranges. Is it any wonder that there are only about three thousand wild dogs left in Africa?

Public participation and, with it, public protest has to be understood as essential, for one reason more than any other – responsibility and vigilance becomes shared. If protest is silenced, as it so often is, it does not mean that it will have disappeared. It might take a long time, but it will be heard again. Anyone with a reasonable sense of political history will vouch for that. Any psychologist will tell you that unexpressed dissatisfaction or anger turns inwards, often predisposing to depression and demotivation in the one who is silenced. However, with time, as

Rilke reminds us, the children will go out in search of the church that the fathers have forgotten. A classic example of this was the fall of the Berlin Wall in 1989. It was impossible for that wall to remain standing – it had already come down in the minds of the younger generation of East Berliners. The forgotten "church" was on the other side of that wall.

DREAMS

A likely objection to the notion of ecological intelligence concerns the significance of dreams. In chapter three, I wrote that it was impossible to understand the admonition of Apollo – know thyself – without an understanding of our dreams. Whether we understand them or not, our dreams are a reality. We have them, or perhaps they have us.

No one who has had the privilege of owning a dog would deny that our canine companions dream. Watching their twitching – often accompanied by plaintive high-pitched calls – as they sleep, one can almost picture them chasing rabbits or squirrels in some ancient field of hide and seek. What need would there be for such an animal to dream, we might ask? Perhaps it is this – to reinforce the survival strategies, the vigilance and the other wild instincts in our otherwise thoroughly domesticated pets. Could this be the reason why human animals dream?

Freud once said that dreams are the royal road to the unconscious and if this is so, as many therapists believe it to be, then it is a road well worth exploring. When viewed from an evolutionary perspective, they can be seen as an essential language of Nature – a primal correspondence. To me, our dreams are poems from the unconscious. They say yes and no. They affect us. They colour our nights and, when we learn to acknowledge them, our days, too. Our dreams are homeostatic and mindful. They modify, motivate, remind, reward, warm, warn and deflate us. They keep us in touch with our feelings.

In this light, it is likely that we dream because we need to. "If sleeping and dreaming do not perform vital biological functions, then they must represent nature's most stupid blunder and most colossal waste of time," say Anthony Stevens and John Price in their thought-provoking book *Evolutionary Psychiatry*. Freud also believed that in addition to their symbolic significance, dreams were "the guardians of sleep and not its disturbers".

Irrespective of how dreams are interpreted, sleep research has shown that our mental health suffers without them. It appears that it is not so much sleep deprivation but dream-phase deprivation that affects us. Dreams are intimately associated with specific chemicals and structures in the mammalian brain as well as with certain phases or periods of sleep. And sleep is not a passive process either, a time in our day when we like to think that the brain switches off. It is precisely the opposite. The brain, through increased nocturnal electro-chemical activity in the evolutionary older brainstem, literally switches on. As a result of this measurable activity, a remarkable physiological phase of sleep, common to all mammals and known as REM or rapid-eye-movement sleep, is initiated. Accompanied by flickering eye-movements as well as a deep relaxing of the muscles, particularly those around the head and neck, REM sleep in humans begins about an hour after sleep onset. Throughout the night it alternates with non-REM sleep, but the alternating patterns vary from person to person and with age. Newborn infants, for instance, spend about half of their sleeping time in REM phase, while the average total in adults is about twenty-five percent.

A significant aspect of REM sleep is that seventy-five percent of our dreaming occurs in this phase and, until fairly recently, many sleep-researchers believed that REM sleep and dreams were synonymous. Based on this belief and on the fact that REM activity is generated in the lowly brainstem, these same scientists saw dreams as mindless or, to put it more politely, as having no intrinsic value. As we shall see, support for this theory is diminishing, for there are those, like the neuro-psychologist Mark Solms, who regard dreams as anything but mindless. "What about non-REM dreams?" he asks, knowing that at least another twenty-five percent of our dreams occur before and after the onset of REM sleep with some of our most vivid dreams occurring before we awaken. His research shows that non-REM dreams are generated not in the brainstem but in the forebrain, giving them a home in the more evolved parts of our brains as well. What is more, the neurochemicals secreted are significantly different from those involved in REM dreams. In REM dreams, the main chemicals are acetyl-choline, nor-epinephrine and serotonin with acetyl-choline in the dominant role. In non-REM dreams, the dominant neurotransmitter is dopamine.

So what, you may ask? What is special about dopamine? Dopamine is the prime biochemical ingredient for seeking, striving, exploratory, predatory and anticipatory behaviour in humans and other animals, and as such, do our dreams have anything to do with seeking behaviour? I believe they do. But for what, in our dreams, are we seeking? Surely, in an evolutionary light, and with the defensive waking ego out of the way, it is for what we anticipate or what we might need to examine, pursue or prioritise in our lives. Could our dreams be part of a persistent, predatory-like search for cohesion and meaning? Often the same theme comes up time and again. It is as if the unconscious, that great wilderness of the psyche, wants us to know something and until we pay attention to them, it will not let us go. Pay attention to your dreams. Honour the gods, said Apollo. Like poetry, they redress the imbalances in our lives. Our psychological integrity and, who knows, even our survival, could depend on them. Freud may have been right when he said that many of our dreams are wish fulfilments – being rewarded with what we cannot have, or for what we are not prepared (for social and for other reasons) in our waking reality. Sometimes, for the sake of what is expedient, our dream world is precisely where the dream should remain. Nevertheless, ignoring them, said Jung, is like refusing to open a letter that has been addressed to you. What follows is an example of how important a dream can be. It was brought to me by one of my patients at a time when he was having to make a choice about a change of career.

Thoroughly bored with his life and with his work, he dreamt that he was relaxing in a dry riverbed, somewhere in the African bush. Suddenly an antelope, chased by a predator, leapt into the sand not far from him. Then came the predator. It was a lion, a huge and powerful specimen,

kicking up columns of gravel as it chased the antelope towards the opposite bank. "I knew that if the lion saw me, then it was all over," he said.
This is exactly what happened. "Turning its attention to me, it advanced
in a low, crouching gait. In a state of fear, I raised my right arm to protect
myself but it was soon upon me". Instead of a mauling, the lion gently
closed its jaws around his arm and the dreamer knew that if he resisted,
it would kill him. It then pulled him out of the riverbed and let him go.
Leaving him unharmed, he watched the great animal sauntering away
until it had disappeared into the surrounding forest. The man awakened,
his heart racing. The dream image stayed with him for days. What was it
trying to tell him? This is what we concluded: the dream was an accurate
reflection of what had become of him in his work. It was as if he was in
a "dry riverbed". There was no flow to his work and to his creativity. He
needed to get out of his situation. He needed to change.

But what role did the lion play in his dream? What wild, archetypal
image of Nature was this? In other words, what did the lion represent
in him? And why did it let him go? Reading up on lion behaviour, my
patient came to understand the lion as an aspect of himself – a representation of what is wild, strong, instinctive and territorial in him –
something that he had neglected. The lion was there to help him to get
back on track with his vocation and, for the sake of his psychological
health, he dare not resist. Animated by the dream image, he made the
change. Accepting a post as a university lecturer brought for him a new-
found sense of creativity and fulfilment. My patient did not choose the
dream. Primed by his psychic situation, it is as if the dream, as a guiding image, chose him.

Do dream images have the same meaning for everyone? The answer
is no. While there may be certain shared cross-cultural interpretations of dream images, strictly speaking, dreams are not interpreted –
they are analysed. A lion or a snake in a dream could represent different
things to different people but that is only a part of the analysis. The most
important part of a dream concerns the context, the timing and the
meaning of the dream for the one who dreams it. In other words, why did

that person have that particular dream at that particular time and what did it mean to him or her? The word analysis is made up of the prefix ana meaning "up", "out", "back", "throughout", and the suffix lysis, which means to "loosen". In the analysis, then, the dream is thoroughly loosened. It is then re-membered, which is to say, it is put together again in a way that is both understandable and meaningful to that individual.

Another important aspect of dream analysis is that the analyst should be aware of what is happening in his or her life when a patient brings a dream into a session. In other words, is the patient's dream intended for me also ... is this a dream that I could have had? Absurd? Why should it be? Are we not a social species? And if we acknowledge that we live in a field of influence or that the unconscious dynamics of the human psyche are historical and shared, would it not make sense that the dreams of those closest to us in our lives and in our work could have something to say about all of us? If this sounds plausible, then what about the dreams of field workers, game rangers, trackers, politicians and policy makers? If dreams are the language of the unconscious, or a language of survival, should we not at least have some interest in what our collective psyches may be telling us?

The difficulty in promoting the language of dreams will be the same as that of promoting poetry as a way of rediscovering ourselves in Nature. The engaged parties, says Seamus Heaney,

> ... are not going to be grateful for a mere image – no matter how inventive or original – of the field of force of which they are a part. They will want poetry [or dreams] to be an exercise of leverage on behalf of their point of view; they will require the entire weight of the redress to come down heavily on their side of the scales. Their general desire will be for simplification.

This is understandable, of course, but poetry and dreams are not intended to simplify. Instead, they should be seen as assisting us to unravel the complex reality which surrounds us and out of which our dreams and poems are generated.

Can you imagine a management meeting that commences, not with a prayer but with the remembering of a dream ... or both?

"And how shall we find the kingdom of heaven?"
the disciples asked.
"Follow the birds and the beasts" came the reply.
"They will show you the way."

St Thomas – The Apocraphyl Gospels

8

RECONCILIATION

I N THE INTRODUCTORY CHAPTER TO THIS BOOK, I WROTE OF A NOTION THAT our sense of self and our sense of place is linked – that our identity is somehow intimately associated with a deep historical sense of kinship with wild places and wild animals and that we are dependent upon them for our psychological health. How we care for them is surely a measure of how we care for each other. Such a notion might help to explain why there was no surprise when two countries with conflicting political ideologies teamed up to free two whales caught up in an ice flow in the Arctic Circle. This happened at the height of the cold war between Russia and the USA in the early 1980s. It does not concern us that the effort cost millions of dollars and the reason it would seem is that our response in such situations is archetypal. For many, the situation grips us. We are compelled to participate, even at a distance and the energy we expend cannot be measured in dollars. We will continue to dig deeply into our resources to help save animals that are endangered or in trouble. And we will do it for the same reasons. We do it for the sake of the animals, but I believe we do it also because we know that at some deep level their fate has something to do with us; that any step toward a reconciliation with the land, with whales, wild dogs and butterflies is a step towards our own healing.

ADAM'S EYE

Perhaps it is no coincidence that the adjectives we use to describe those occasional deep feelings of connection with animals and with the land are often the very ones that best describe the phenomenon of healing – indescribable, unpredictable, unforgettable.

The big question of course is: can this reconciliation be facilitated or will it remain a series of unpredictable one-off events? I believe it can be nurtured but it is going to require a profound change in our attitude towards the Human-Nature relationship. Earlier, I made a number of suggestions that could help us, namely, to stop speaking of the Earth being in need of healing; to become more evolutionary and psychologically minded and to nurture a language that is healing. However, it is going to require something else. It is going to require that we develop what the analyst James Hillman refers to as Adam's eye – a way of seeing animals and landscape beyond human parallels and the usual laboratory explanations – beyond grasping at the meaning and metaphor of the animal. It is an aesthetic eye, he says, "a perception for which psychology is yet to train its senses". It is an eye that promotes survival; that excites the emotions; that takes us to the unexplored edges of the human-animal interface and to the realisation that *everything* is intelligent. It is a process that begins when we are grateful for the mere presence of the animal. It ends when you know the animal in yourself.

But why Adam? Put yourself into the skin of the first allegorical man on this one: "And out of the ground, the lord God formed every beast and every fowl of the air; and brought them unto Adam to see what he would call them; and whatsoever Adam called every living creature, that was the name thereof." How would you have responded had you been asked to name the animals? Where and how would you have begun? Surely you would need to know something about your own animal nature. In this poem, I salute the Adam in us.

> Long before the message
> of a Word made flesh;
> long before his loss of innocence
> and the naming of his soul,
> a man of clay and a lonely heart
> gave names to his animal flesh.

Pulled
by twisting threads,
he found his way to the scales of dawn,
to his open gills,
to the turn of the tide of blood
and the crossing back to air.

Naked
in a long necked night
of re-membering,
he sloped his way toward the light,
he raised his arm to a passing whale,
his thoughts took flight,
by then ... he'd named
Himself.

If we are serious about rediscovering ourselves in Nature, we all need to take that journey. But we each have to do it in our own way. To know ourselves we have to know our own animal nature first. We have to wrestle the "beasts" in us, as Adam did. Why? In order that our animal energy can be transformed – that it can be given a human face. We have to learn how to say yes and no to the crocodile, the fox, the lion and the bear in us. It is a priceless journey.

However, you have to be willing to be disturbed. To enter into the wild places of the Earth is to enter the wild places of the human psyche at the same time – it is both a reaching out and a homecoming. As happens in the wild, you may need a guide – someone who knows the terrain, who can read the territory, who thinks like a shaman and who knows when it is time to turn back. You may need someone who can help you to bring your wild images back into the everyday-world and to embrace them.

In almost every traditional culture, animals have been and remain the guiding spirits of the shamans, those rare individuals whose role, more than anything else, has been that of defending the psychic integrity of their communities. They are the men and women who know the language of the animals and of the land and because of this, they know the terrain and the animals in the psyche of their people. "We are part of the Earth and it is a part of us," wrote Chief Seattle in 1855 in a letter to the president in Washington.

> We know the sap which comes through the trees as we know the blood that courses through our veins. Every part of the Earth is sacred to my people, every shining pine needle, every sandy shore, every mist in the dark woods, every meadow, every humming insect. The rivers are our brothers. They quench our thirst. They carry our canoes and they feed our children. So you must give to the river the kindness you would give any brother.

And then there are these insightful lines from a poem by Pablo Neruda, "I'm Aware of the Earth's Skin". He is reminding us of the core of our nature:

> No one can be named Pedro,
> no one is Rosa or Maria,
> all of us are dust or sand,
> all of us are rain in the rain.
> They have talked to me of Venezuelas,
> of Paraguays and Chiles,
> I don't know what they're talking about:
> I'm aware of the EARTH's skin
> and I know that it doesn't have a name.

We are in dire need of modern-day shamans, men and women who are aware of the Earth's skin, or, as Mercia Eliade, the former head of the History of Religions at the University of Chicago, wrote in 1964, "we are in dire need of modern day specialists in the sacred".

ASKING PERMISSION

There is another requirement for the reconciliation that we seek. It has to do with honouring the gods – we have to ask permission to do so. To ask permission is not only an act of respect, it is an art. It begins when you acknowledge that every encounter with Nature is a dual experience; that it involves the intelligence of the other; and that the other may be more intelligent than you – that you may be the one who is lost. What do you do when you are lost, when you can't find your way through your world?, "Stand still!" says the poet David Wagoner in his magnificent poem, "Lost":

> Stand still!
> The trees ahead and the bushes beside you ...
> They are not lost.
> Remember, wherever you are
> Is also called here
> And you must treat it like a powerful stranger;
> Must ask permission to know it
> And be known.
> Listen!
> The forest breathes ... it whispers
> I made this place around you
> And if you leave, you may come back again
> Saying "Here!"
> No two trees are the same to raven
> No two branches the same to wren
> But ... if what a tree or a branch does is lost on you
> Then you are truly lost.
> Stand still!
> The forest knows where you are,
> Let it find you.

Wagoner's words remind us that there is a "critical distance" between all living things, an invisible territory that must never be taken for granted. Be mindful of it for it is real. It is dynamic, contextual, unpredictable and powerful. It is a space that is filled with the ancient chemistry of yes and no – the first language.

To enter into the space of another without permission, be it the land, the sea or that of an animal, is to violate that space. How do you ask permission from the land? You do it in the same way that you ask permission to enter the space of a patient, a friend, a lover or a stranger. You take care. You "listen" to the intelligence of the other. You pay attention. You listen – feelingly.

In the African wilderness, as in all the wild places of the world, to listen to the land is to "listen" to the wind, to its direction, to its touch, to its scents – the promise of rain, the perfume of spring, the pheromones of decay, excrement and spray. It is to heed the caution that you may be upwind of that which is "listening" to you. It is to listen to the signatures in the sand and to what the birds, the squirrels the baboons and the antelope have to say. The alarm calls of these creatures are for the same predators that unsettle the human animal. The animals tell us when to look up, down and around. They also tell us when to go away.

When asked by Barry Lopez what he did when he visited a new place, the Innuit hunter answered: "I listen. That's all. I listen to what the land is saying. I walk around in it and strain my senses in appreciation of it for a long time, before I myself, ever speak a word." This man believed that if entered in such a respectful manner, the land would open to him, said Lopez. This is the art of asking permission.

Stand still. Listen. Be patient. Try and make sure that the space between you and the other is safe and containing for you both. As practised in analytical therapy, "begin by giving a free-floating attention to the encounter," says the London-based psychoanalyst Eric Rayner. Keep a close eye on your reactions. Remember you are in a shared field of influence. Engage yourself in what could be called a primal correspondence – the way a parent, on a non-verbal level, is receptive to what her infant is trying to say. Be deeply receptive to what is rising and falling around you – the intentions, the emotions and the needs of the other. Develop a sixth sense, what Aristotle called a common sense where the primary qualities of intensity, motion, rest, unity, form and number are represented in abstract form and translated into *any one of our senses*.

Try and see yourself through the eyes of the other. Be utterly present and open to the guiding potential of whatever impressions or images may emerge, mindful that you do not know what is going to happen next and that what you bring to the encounter could be rejected. As the poet Ortega y Gasset puts it, "create an attention that does not consist in riveting itself to the presumed but consists precisely in not presuming anything and avoiding inattentiveness". In other words, be especially careful of trying to understand the behaviour of the animal according to your own needs and expectations. As Lopez reminds us, this is an old trap and to fall for it is to end up knowing very little about the animal at all. Even worse, it is to deny the animal. Animals do not have an ego consciouness as humans do. If they did, then prepare yourself for what the poet Rilke wrote in this verse from the Eighth Duiono Elegy:

> If the animal moving toward us so securely
> in a different direction had our kind of
> consciousness -, it would wrench us around and drag us
> along its path. But it feels its life as boundless,
> unfathomable, and without regard
> to its own condition: pure, like its outward gaze.
> And where we see the future, it sees all time
> and itself within all time, forever healed.

Get back to basics. Know something about the behaviour of the animal other – its preferences, its territory and its threat displays. Sometimes the permission you seek may not be granted. If so, respect the refusal. Back off.

Pay careful attention, therefore, to detail – the swish of a tail, the angle of the head, the inclined ear, the positioning of the feet. Appreciate the timing of the encounter. Were you there first or did you stumble into the space of the one that confronts you? With elephants, for example, to be there first invariably ends up with them giving you a wide berth. When the situation is reversed, be prepared to do the same for them. Watch out if you don't. Try not to surprise them. Note the time of day. Not all animals see well in twilight. Keep the flashlight low. Try to understand the dolphin-ness, the elephant-ness and the heron-ness of the one who is with you. Ask these questions of yourself: am I too close, too big, too quick? Have I inadvertently crossed the critical line? Ask of the other: "What is your way?" And then, "Can I share it with you?"

Don't be too hasty to discard or interpret the images and feelings that may arise, for they can present in any number of ways – a pattern, a shape, a sound, a memory, a feeling. Sometimes the encounter brings a deep sense of familiarity and other times a silence that is both humble and foetal; it may be a sense that this is delicate; that it will take time; that there is no hurry. With time, you will begin to find that your inter-pretations will become a lot more appropriate and meaningful. And when the encounter is over, say thank you.

TO BECOME THE ANIMAL

What does the traditional hunter mean when he says you must *become* the animal? In its most practical sense, if you are living in wolf country, to "become" a wolf is to know how to "see" like a wolf, says Barry Lopez. It is to know how to find your way home in polar darkness and in a whiteout. It is "to be comfortable without that one thing indis-pensable to a Western navigator – an edge". It is to have an affinity for relationships rather than boundaries, to read the wind, the contours of the land and the language of the snow underfoot. To "become" that ani-mal, borrowing words from the naturalist and author David Abram, is to "turn inside out, to loosen the psyche from its confinement within a strictly human sphere". It is to discover that intelligence is not peculiar to the human animal, but a property of the Earth and of every living thing, where each terrain, each ecology, each animal seems to have its own particular intelligence.

To become one with the other is to be receptive to a one-to-one exchange that is physical, cognitive, interpersonal but most of all, intuitive. It is what Rayner refers to in psychotherapy as "matching activity". Emphasising the intuitive aspect of the exchange is an acknowledgement that the way we perceive and translate our correspondence with others is mostly subliminal – we are not aware that we are doing it. We focus on things, yes, but we are essentially unconscious scanners, taking in information that is not censored by the ego and which, from time to time, is perceived on a subjective level as a "hunch", a "resonance" or a sense that something is happening "out there". And, as the following example will show, it can happen while you are asleep. It is an example that is supported by many of the wilderness guides with whom I have worked:

During the months that I spent in Botswana's Linyanti wilderness, consolidating the content of this book, I was often awakened at night by elephants, lions and sometimes by leopards, not because they were making a noise, but because of the silence. Sitting up and peering through the gauze netting of our tent, I would then see them – the dark silhouettes of the grey giants on their way to the river. Sometimes there was nothing to see, but the morning would confirm the reason why I had been awakened. There, in front of the tent, like an open diary, were the records of the nocturnal visitors. Perhaps a leopard and, later, a lion had come and gone. My internal "antennae" were active. Of course, there were other nights when the sounds of breaking branches or the thundering roar of lions could awaken the dead. However, thank heavens for the safety of the tent. Without it I would have slept very poorly.

But what about mismatching – the sensing of a relationship where the "chemistry" is absent, or where the contact is premature or threatening? If to ask permission to enter the space of another is an art, then the awareness of mismatching is part of that art. This, too, is intuitive. Matching and mismatching are essential aspects of a process in which neurochemical/archetypal responses of withdrawal, flight, approach, challenge, co-operation and delayed gratification can be triggered. Sometimes mismatching has much to do with one's own sense of vulnerability. Sometimes you simply don't have time to ask permission. What do you do when there is no neutrality in the space between you and the other? What then? Sometimes, the only choice you have is to let the wildness in you meet the wildness out there – head on. An example of this comes from an encounter my wife and I had with a spotted hyena.

One new moon night, while camping in the Savuti Channel in the Linyanti, I found myself suddenly awake. Next to me, my wife was sitting bolt upright, listening. Out of the dark night we heard the footsteps of something very close. In an instant, we simultaneously roared our territorial call: "HAY!" Reaching for my flashlight I quickly picked up the eyes and the shape of the intruder. Having smelled the leftovers of our supper, a spotted hyena had come to investigate. Reflecting on the incident, I was intrigued by the explosive, anxious, animal-like nature of my response. Where did it come from? Who knows. What I do know is that it was loud, it was natural, it was territorial, and it was aggressive. I believe it was coming from the depths of an ancient mammalian bloodline, or, if you prefer, an ancient evolutionary Self.

INTENTION

We all know that our domestic animals somehow "see" through our deceptive sweetness and avoid us or mysteriously disappear when our intentions are to get them to a vet. It is also well known in the wild that animals quickly learn the difference between a hunter and a photographer and that even a photographer can be threatening.

Researching the sometimes baffling ability of humans and animals to anticipate other people's intentions, a group of Italian neurophysiologists at the University of Parma may have stumbled on to what they believe to be a key to this mystery. They have described in humans and in our primate cousins a new class of nerve cells called mirror neurons. These remarkable cells are situated in the pre-motor cortex of the frontal lobe. Studying macaque monkeys, they noted that this particular area of the brain becomes active not only during certain motor tasks such as reaching out for food, or moving to pick up specific objects, but they also become active in monkeys that are *observing* the ones that are performing the action. In effect, the observer unconsciously mirrors the action of the performer. Upon closer examination, they discovered that the patterns of the brain waves were not only specific to the task but were shared by both the performer and the observer. In other words, you could expect a different anticipatory brain wave in an animal observing a man picking up a camera to that of a man reaching for a gun.

Linked to memories and emotions surrounding similar tasks, actions and situations, these mirror neurones appear to be essential to the way we anticipate and understand the intentions of the other. They are therefore essential for what we call learned behaviour. In humans, the mirror neurones are situated close to Broca's Area, that part of the brain responsible for executive speech. Could mirror neurone activity be the neurological precursors of speech and language – an evolutionary older function than speech itself? Are they the neurological triggers of the alarm calls and contact calls that we share with all red-blooded creatures? But there is more. The fact that they appear to be firing in sympathy in both the observer and the performer suggests that they could be linked to the neurobiology of empathy, compassion and what has been frequently referred to in this book as the art of "getting into the skin of the other". The poets, like Rilke (in these lines from "Turning Point"), have known about mirror neurons for ages:

> Animals trusted him, stepped
> into his open look, grazing,
> and the imprisoned lions stared in
> as if into an incomprehensible freedom ...

There is no doubt that some people have a way with animals. Notwithstanding the bonds that build up over time between animals and their handlers, mutual trust, sometimes immediate, has much to do with the demeanour, the attitude and the intention of the animal handlers themselves. The following remarkable and well-documented story is an example of what I mean. It involved a Botswana-based American safari operator, Randall Moore, and a wounded elephant bull in the Pilanesburg Game Reserve in the Northern Province of South Africa. The wound had been caused by a deep hippopotamus bite to one of its legs which had then become infected, resulting in a need for surgical intervention. The animal was darted, anaesthetised and the infected area appropriately treated. The wound did not heal immediately, however, and it was soon realised that several interventions would be needed. The surgeon was faced with a dilemma. On the one hand the animal needed to be treated but on the other there was a serious risk to the elephant if it was to undergo repeated anaesthetics. Moore, who had released this animal from captivity into the wild twelve years previously, was called in from his elephant-back safari operation in Botswana to help. To the astonishment of all involved, the elephant immediately recognised Moore's call and approached him as if to greet him. Moore, in turn, expressed his intention to help in the way that he "spoke" to the animal, telling it what was required. As if permission had been granted, the man was able to treat the animal's wound and, over a period of several days, the elephant would stand and quietly allow the wound to be bathed and dressed.

In another fascinating story about animal-human communication, Heinz Koors, a veterinary surgeon involved in an elephant relocation programme near the Kruger National Park, was asked why "his" elephants seemed to be so relaxed while those handled by another operator kept breaking out of their enclosures. He answered: "I speak to the matriarch in the group and ask her not to break out." When I asked him to confirm this story, he confessed that he couldn't be specific about it. However, his reputation had preceded him and a fellow wild-life manager supported the popular version of Koors's particular gift.

Does this imply that there is some special technique for communicating with elephants or other animals? I suspect there is, but it is not something one can learn from a book. I believe, even if it is on a subconscious level, you would have to *know* the animals with whom you are relating, and if they happen to be elephants, you would have to know the "elephant" in you.

To me, the aim of human-to-animal communication is clear. It is not about trying to get the animals to like you, or to have them at your beck and call. Instead, through body language, tone of voice, or even music (on several occasions I have inflicted the gentle strumming of a guitar on elephant bulls as well as spotted hyenas), it is to let them know that you mean no harm; that you want to learn not only about them, but from them. I believe it works. Whether they warmed to it or not, I don't know, but on two separate occasions I had a hyena, at less than 30 metres, respond to the strumming with its characteristic contact call. On each occasion the hyena then moved on. The elephant bulls, on the other hand, would often stand quite still, listening, the base of their trunks expanding and contracting in what I believe is an infra-sound response to the musical strings. I was subsequently delighted to read, in Douglas Chadwick's book *The Fate Of The Elephants*, a report by long-time elephant researcher Joyce Poole about elephants "drawn to the strains of guitar music issuing from camp some evenings". She observed how, compared with other elephant incursions into the campsite, no one bothered to chase these elephants away.

In a poignant and humbling record of a piece of research in which the importance of the seeking of permission is powerfully evident, the University of Michigan primatologist, Barbara Smuts, describes what she has learned about herself from her encounters with baboons.

I was lucky to be accepted by the animals as a mildly interesting, harmless companion, permitted to travel amongst them. Under the guise of scientific research, I was in the company of expert guides – baboons who could spot a predator a mile away and who seemed to possess a sixth sense for the proximity of snakes. Abandoning myself to their far superior knowledge, I moved as a humble disciple, learning from masters about being an African anthropoid. Thus I became (or, rather, regained my ancestral right to be) an animal, moving instinctively through a world that felt (because it was) like my ancient home. The baboons stubbornly resisted my feeble but sincere attempts to convince them that I was nothing more than a detached observer, a neutral object they could ignore. Right from the start, they knew better, insisting that I was, like them, a social subject vulnerable to the demands and rewards of relationship. The deepest lessons came when I found myself sharing the being of a baboon, because other baboons were treating me like one ...

What I see as a creative or critical distance between one's self and the other, Smuts sees as an "invisible line" that defines the personal space between each troop member, a space that expands and contracts, depending on the circumstances. Anyone involved in the dynamics of one-on-one psychotherapy will know about that "invisible" line.

Do we still need reminding that we have within us millions of years of life as corresponding, reflecting beings? We must not forget this. This, in essence, was Smuts' secret. She stopped thinking about what to do and instead "surrendered to instinct, not as mindless, reflexive action, but rather as action rooted in an ancient primate legacy of embodied knowledge." She learned how to ask permission to be with the baboons. And it was granted.

One of the most sobering experiences I have ever had in the wild occurred on an open plain in Botswana's Okavango Delta. I was guiding a group of tourists when a herd of elephants two kilometres away from us began to run away from us. Having picked up the scent and sight of humans, the reaction was one of obvious mistrust. The reason for this was clear. The area I was in had been a hunting concession less than a year previously. Who could blame the elephants? Our timing was wrong, and so was our sensing of the critical distance between us. As it is with humans, experiential memory runs deep in the animal kingdom. It did not matter that our intentions were benign. Human beings had lost the elephants' trust and our group had unwittingly crossed the "invisible line". It would take a long time for other humans to re-establish the trust. We would need to get to know that place all over again.

Thomas, the Saint, has urged us to follow the birds and the beasts, for they will show us the way. Is this really applicable? I believe it is and what follows confirms this belief. It concerns the recreating of ancient migration routes of large animals like elephants. The question is where, exactly, should these corridors be established? Iain Douglas-Hamilton of the Save the Elephant Foundation and, more recently, Michael Chase of the Elephants Without Boundaries project in Botswana, have come up with a brilliant answer – let the elephants decide. Let the animals show us the way. Absurd? Not at all. As a result of his outstanding radio tracking studies on the seasonal paths and patterns of migrating elephants, Douglas-Hamilton has been able to tell us more than we previously understood about elephant migrations, the directions they wish to take, as well as the land areas in which they are comfortable or uncomfortable – they move at high speed through these uncomfortable areas. Not surprisingly, these very areas are the ones that are in close proximity to human habitation and to hunters. Who could argue that these elephants were not telling us something? Should we not listen to them? And could we take this work further? How about a north-south and an east-west elephant corridor through Central and Southern Africa, with the elephants showing us the way? And remember, where elephants go, many other animals follow. I can see the heads shaking and I can understand why. Veterinary fences and civil conflict will make it impractical. It will be too expensive, too political, too risky and it is going to take a long time to implement. Political and economic logistics aside, I believe it is an idea and a dream that we must not give up on. After all, are we not trying to open the "corridors" in the human psyche?

In conclusion, what, if anything, does the correspondence between humans and animals mean to us? Lopez answers this question, albeit cryptically: "If you are trying to fathom wolves," he says, " I think it can mean almost everything." He could have been referring equally to elephants, leopards or hyenas. To understand this correspondence will be a huge step towards rediscovering ourselves in Nature and to seeing the world, at last, as a mirror. We will come face to face with ourselves. It will certainly bring us face to face with one of the most emotive issues of the new millennium – the ethics of recreational and trophy hunting of wild animals.

And only then, when I have learned enough
I will go to watch the animals, and let
something of their composure slowly guide
into my limbs; will see my own existence
deep in their eyes...

Rainer Maria Rilke

9

THE KEEPING OF THE ZOO

A S A YOUNG BOY GROWING UP IN PRESENT DAY ZAMBIA, I LIVED IN A neighbourhood where it was not uncommon for people to display kudu horns or elephant tusks in their homes. My uncle kept a lion skin, with its snarling head attached, spread out on the floor of his verandah. He didn't shoot the animal, but he was nevertheless honoured to accept the trophy as a gift from a professional hunter. No one thought anything of it, except that my uncle, years later, removed it from its position of display. Somehow, it was no longer appropriate, he said. It was about this time, prior to entering medical school, that I spent a short period as a farm manager in Zimbabwe. The owner of the farm was a man who loved hunting. Suspended on the walls of the family room in his home were the heads of at least three of the "big five". Other heads included that of a spotted hyena as well as a variety of antelopes. Today, that same farm is a wild animal sanctuary where tourists can walk among elephants, rhino and the kin of those antelopes that adorned the walls of the family room. Today, that man is no longer a hunter.

What makes a professional or recreational hunter suddenly lower his gun, no longer able to pull the trigger on the animal in his sights? What causes the sudden wave of tiredness that makes him say: "That's enough," turning his attention instead to taking photographs of the animals and to protecting them? Has the hunter gone soft, or has he become strong? Perhaps hunters simply get tired of their way of life, the novelty wears off, the animal-human contest becomes hollow or they ultimately prefer to see the animal alive. Wild animals know when they are being hunted and the hunters know it. On the other hand, could there be a more complex reason for why some hunters put away their guns. Was it something about the creature in their sights? Was it the sheer elegance of the animal or perhaps the look in its eye? Was there a deep, unarticulated realisation that it is not the way of Nature to kill anything for amusement?

These are debatable reasons for laying down a weapon, but there is one more, a less obvious reason, that I would like to propose. My proposal is in defence of what I would like to call the "authentic" hunters of the world. From the "bushmen" to the likes of the early twentieth century hunter Frederick Courtney Selous, after whom the Selous National Park in Tanzania is named, these are the hunters who know and understand the behaviour of every animal they hunt – from lizards to lions. The arrows or bullets they use are associated with the self-preserving hormone adrenalin. These hunters are not dependent on trackers, trucks or geographical positioning systems. They know the tracks of the animals, their terrain, which ones to kill, which ones to leave alone and, more importantly, they know that crucial "invisible line" which, once crossed, is to betray an unwritten pact between the hunter and the hunted: that the contest be fair and *necessary*. Grounded in experience and a deep sense of respect for the animal, this awareness is the defining characteristic separating the authentic from the unauthentic hunter. These hunters are among the finest guides, naturalists and wilderness educators I know and they have good reason to regard themselves as genuine conservationists. Few of them remain and as Map Ives, a former professional hunter turned professional environmentalist, ruefully observes, "they are a dying breed". Could it be that these hunters have put down their guns because of an ethical imperative – they have become increasingly ill-at-ease, repelled by their association with, or worse still, their financial dependence on, unauthentic hunters, especially modern trophy hunters and the industry that supports them?

To me, the trophy hunter is the opposite of the hunter I have just described. Because they own guns, know how to shoot and they love being in the wild, they would like to be seen as authentic, but a love of the wild, and of guns, is not enough. With rare exceptions, even among professional hunters, they have little more than a superficial knowledge of how the animals, the birds and the landscape are intertwined. Instead, their mission is clear – they have come to kill the animal of their choice and they have paid good money to do so. What is more, there must be as little physical risk to themselves as possible. Supported by an industry that practically guarantees their safety and their kill, they know little, if anything, about that "invisible line". When their bullets are fired, they are associated not so much with adrenalin as with testosterone, as I will show. Governed by time constraints and heavily reliant on trackers and sophisticated weaponry, for the unauthentic hunter the trophy, rather than the human-animal interaction, is paramount.

There is presently an unprecedented groundswell of public antipathy towards recreational and trophy hunting and it is coming from all corners – from animal rights movements and those who simply espouse animal welfare and protection, to conservation biologists and those same hunters who have downed their guns. Hunting – and particularly trophy hunting – has become more of a moral and ethical issue than ever before. In spite of rebound protest from so-called "ethical" hunters, one of the reasons for the growing mistrust, in addition to certain highly questionable present-day hunting activities, is that Nature's backlashes are inevitable and usually slow. In other words, much of the antipathy is inherited from the past. From Gordon Cumming in the19th Century to the well-documented escapades of Theodore Roosevelt, Ernest Hemingway and many others, the image and ethics of the archetypal trophy hunter is not as admirable as we were sometimes led to imagine. What these men may have been admired for, or been proud of, in their time, we would be ashamed of today. Some would call it carnage. In their defence, and it is a poor one, it could be argued that they were less informed about the science of ecology and evolution than we are today. However, I believe, in the words of Oedipus: "they should have known."

As we are witnessing now, it could be as much as the sixth or seventh generation later who are left to repair the damage of the forefathers. It is no wonder, therefore, that the non-hunting public today are mistrusting and critical of modern hunters. As for the hunters, it is not enough to change their vocabulary, for example, what was once the Botswana Professional Hunters Association, is now sceptically known as the Botswana Wildlife Management Association. It is going to take time to believe in the new hunting terminology of ethical versus unethical hunting. Nobody can convincingly describe himself as authentic or ethical – he has to be known to be so, consistently. In other words, you cannot be your own judge. It may be to their credit that they are reconsidering the impact of their choice of lifestyle but it is not going to help their cause when they refer to their critics as "vociferous minorities ... sensationalists ... self-styled, pseudo-environmentalists ... bent on imposing their intolerant views on society" as was written by Gerard R Damm (*Africa Geographic*, February 2003), Whether it be the voice or pen of the hunter or that of their critics, contempt usually says more about the one who has it than the ones to whom it is directed.

What follows, then, is not a demand but rather an appeal to those who continue to justify any form of hunting outside of food and food production to reconsider its history, its validity and its ethic. It is an appeal to read the message of the thorns of the zizyphus – to remember where we have come from.

The roots of hunting have a remote origin in the psyche of the human animal and as the psychologist William James wrote in 1896, "it is just because human bloodthirstiness is such a primitive part of us that it is so hard to eradicate, especially where a fight or a hunt is promised as part of the fun." But is the hunting of a wild animal in our blood? Is it an instinct? In defence of their sport, recreational and trophy hunters often urge us to believe that it is so; that it is linked to deep-seated predatory drives; that it confirms that human beings are the evolutionary champions of the animal food chain and that for a man to be a "man", he must hunt.

I will argue that the roots of trophy hunting are in the evolution of culture rather than biology; that the hunting of wild animals is learned behaviour and that as the context changes, what we have learned can not only become inappropriate, but maladaptive.

First of all, we must not confuse hunting with the instinct to protect and to provide. Secondly, we must learn the difference between an instinct and a habit. If the hunting of wild animals were an instinct, then surely it would have to be shared by everyone. Instead, because recreational and trophy hunting is largely a first-world practice, we would do well to reflect on the The Fund for Animals report of 2000, which records that in America, fourteen million people hunt compared with sixty-two million who practice "less consumptive activities such as bird watching, hiking and photography" – to say nothing of the growing number of people who oppose hunting altogether. If anything, it is the aesthetic, "less consumptive" activities, that appear to be "instinctive". To me, the latter group are evidence of what it means to unlearn or to redirect old attitudes. The gun has been replaced by a camera; telescopic sites by long-range lenses; the bullet by a film or memory chip and the "trophy" remains alive.

Looking back on our early beginnings, it is likely that one factor more than any other was responsible for our progression from individualistic foragers to collective scavengers and then hunters – the quality of our diet. The protein derived from the eating of small mammals, reptiles and the scavenging on carcasses was not enough. We needed more animal protein and it needed to be fresh. Bone marrow and organ meat became increasingly important as "brain food", necessitating that we invent more sophisticated ways of obtaining it. As human animals we did not come blessed with the ability to out-smell, out-see or to out-run the animal meat we desperately needed. Instead, in conjunction with a remarkable increase in the size and neural circuitry of the hominin forebrain, our ancestors learned to out-think their prey. They formed hunting alliances, the equivalent of today's goal-oriented economic and political alliances.

There is little doubt, when viewing the stone tools of *Homo erectus*, that he was a more sophisticated hunter than his smaller-brained predecessor, *Homo habilis*. But there was more to it than just tool making. The need for meat and marrow, combined with the neurological equipment to plan its acquisition, predisposed the species to a huge leap in the sophistication of animal tracking – checking, comparing, collating, interpreting, testing and re-testing – a process akin to modern scientific thinking. It almost goes without saying that to have been a successful hunter one had to be a successful tracker, but even that was not enough. Not only did the hunters have to learn to read the signatures in the sand, they had to learn the ways of the animals, their applied anatomy, physiology and their behaviour. They had to learn about the environment in which the animals moved and lived and about the seasons of water, wind and fire. They had to learn how to put the elements to their advantage, and finally, because the emotions of fear and anxiety were always with them, they had to learn how to interpret and prioritise their own emotional responses to threat and danger.

In his book *Affective Neuroscience*, the neurobiologist Jaak Panskepp writes the following:

> As the humanoid brain developed enough cortex to think and to elaborate complex ideas, hunting became an acquired practice of the human lifestyle. Humans eventually developed the habit of stalking prey and eating meat as do some present-day male chimpanzees in the wild. It is likely however that this thread of character emerged independently of the intense and persistent carnivorous hunting urges of the cats and dogs of the ancient plains.

Shaped by the environment, by necessity and aided by an intelligence that made it workable, hunting became an adapted form of what neurobiologists refer to as seeking behaviour – in this case, the seeking of food taking priority over the seeking of companionship, attachment and approval.

In summary, the seeking of food is one thing, how it is achieved is another. We had to learn how to hunt and it did not only apply to the human animal. An example of what I mean can be seen in the food-seeking behaviour of baboons and otters. Try raising a baboon and an otter in captivity and then, after three years, releasing them into the wild. Within an hour, we could expect the otter to have caught a fish. Instinct. The baboon, on the other hand, will not have a clue about what or what not to eat. It would have to learn the hard way that a scorpion (a wild delicacy), for instance, has to be de-tailed before eating it.

Hunting, as essential as it has been to human survival, has to be understood as an important part of the *learning* curve of human culture. And yet, precisely because of its cultural significance, there are reasons other than the learned skills of acquiring food and skins for blankets and clothing why hunting continues to hold its appeal.

Historically, for communities like the Kalahari "bushmen", the many hunting tribes of Africa, the Nunamuit people of Alaska and the traditional Native Americans, hunting was never simply an act of throwing a spear, pulling the bowstring or aiming a gun. It was also central to healing rituals and to the initiatory rites of passage of young adolescents into manhood and womanhood. Hunting, then, was also a symbolic act. To face and to kill a wild animal was about proving oneself in one's community, that a young man, for instance, could face his fears and that he could provide food, skins and ornaments for his people. The trophy was the evidence of a man's skill, courage and prowess. To succeed was to gain wide-ranging approval and privileges from one's peers and from one's community. In many instances, hunting in this form was part of a mate-selection ritual. Today there are few areas in the world where such traditional lifestyles prevail. However, the need to prove oneself remains. It is part of our nature and while there are other ways of proving oneself, approval, as we shall see, is central to the psychological dynamics of trophy hunting.

THE PSYCHO-BIOLOGY OF HUNTING

When hunters take aim at an animal, how do they divorce themselves from personal feelings of negativity, especially the feelings aroused by the thought of the distress the animal may be experiencing?

To protect the ego from being overwhelmed by negative feelings, the hunter becomes desensitised.

Desensitisation is part of the process of denial, an important but complex defence mechanism of the human ego. In the process of blocking our feelings, we become hardened to the predicament and the feelings of the other. As in any form of indoctrination – a less polite word for required learning – the earlier the desensitisation occurs, the more reinforced it becomes. In his book *Body Count: The Death Toll in America's War on Wildlife*, N Phelps reminds us that 89% of American hunters began hunting before they were nineteen years old; 69% before they were sixteen and 54% before they were thirteen. What makes the process of desensitisation in young people so easy is that it is socially sanctioned, albeit by an inner circle of family members and friends. Promoted in the name of kinship, belonging and the upholding of traditional values, the child and the young adolescent can hardly resist the call to hunt, for as we know, it is only in late adolescence and early adulthood that young people begin to re-examine the value systems of society and of their kin.

Another form of denial is dissociation – the emotionally expedient act of distancing oneself from unpleasant or threatening situations. As in the socially sanctioned madness of war, the hunter, like the soldier, dissociates himself from the trauma. A traumatic event, then becomes dramatic. The trophy hunter is lulled into a complex yet absurd process of self-deception. The animal, the other, becomes the threat, the projected villain ... the enemy. For the trophy hunter to maintain this deception the stuffed animal in his home is invariably made to look dangerous. The implication is clear – the hunter is perceived as having shot the animal in self-defence.

A further, well-used form of denial is justification – the act of convincing oneself that what one is doing is right, that there are good reasons to believe in certain traditions and to behave in specific ways. By aligning their activities to biological drives, hunters in general find little difficulty justifying their sport. As we are beginning to find out, this alignment is not biologically driven, but a learned behaviour.

However, there is another reason given for trophy hunting that is often overlooked. Once again, it stems not so much from biological evolution, but from cultural evolution. It is linked to the ancient, misguided belief that wild animals are dangerous. It is well known that those who are attracted to danger, more especially to the psycho-social challenge that comes with high risk behaviour, will travel great distances to confront and to overcome it and to bring back the trophy. I will give my reasons for why they do this, but before doing so, we would do well to remember that the "big five" (elephant, rhinoceros, buffalo, lion and leopard) is hunting terminology. They are so named because they are the most dangerous when they are threatened, wounded, when they are protecting their young and when their escape routes are foiled. It is well documented that, with rare exceptions, every one of these animals will steer clear and even run away from the full profile of humans. When their behaviour is understood, the "big five" are not dangerous, or, if you prefer, they are as dangerous as you and I would be in the same circumstances. It is the hunter who creates the danger.

But why would anyone want to have an animal's head on his wall? The answer, I believe, is not difficult to find. There are fairly plausible psychological reasons, one of them being the deep human need for approval. From war medals through university certificates, sporting laurels and the heads of wild animals, our exhibits say the same thing – they are our displays of talent, achievement, acceptance and prowess. Sigmund Freud, by the way, would have referred to these displays as phallic, which, as we shall see, is not that far from the truth.

The need for approval is both primal and necessary. We admire people who set goals and who achieve them. We admire those who turn adversity into something of value. These are our role models and our leaders. However, in today's ecological climate it is extremely difficult to approve or admire anyone who kills an animal for the sport. It is difficult to justify, as proposed by the same hunter (*Africa Geographic* February 2003) that "the reason we hunt is for that *special feeling*" (my italics). What kind of a feeling is he talking about? When examined carefully, we find that it is a feeling that is linked to the aggressively competitive nature of hunting itself and, as we shall see, it is primarily a male thing (96% of the members of the Safari Club International – the biggest hunting society in the world – are males).

Aggression and assertion are not only linked, but evolutionary significant – without them we would not have been able to compete effectively for environmental resources. Let's take a closer look at the neurobiological basis of aggression and why men are intrinsically more aggressive than women. To do this, we need to return to the almond-shaped nucleus in the temporal lobe of our brains – the amygdala.

This little structure, apart from being activated by emotionally charged situations, is one of several nuclei involved in seeking or exploratory behaviour. It triggers the feelings associated with curiosity, reward, anticipation and other appetitive states such as hunger and thirst. In both men and women, the amygdala is active in power play and dominance behaviour. It is also involved in what is referred to as predatory or dispassionate "cold aggression" as well as its opposite, the "hot aggression" associated with avenge and revenge. However, there is an important difference between the sexes – these nuclei are significantly larger and more active in men than in women, even when we are asleep. From primates to rodents, the activity in this nucleus indicates that males show more concern for victory, winning, power and dominance than females.

But how does this translate to trophy hunting and to that "special feeling" that the trophy hunter cannot do without? As it is in any sport, it has to do with competition and the joy of winning. It has been conclusively shown that victory in a variety of forms – in sexual and social competition, on tennis courts, through academic degrees and from military ventures to hunting – is associated with increased blood-levels of the sexual hormone testosterone. With it comes the feeling of prowess and dominance. Losers, on the other hand, exhibit declined levels of the hormone. Combined with other morphine-like chemicals involved in competitive play, testosterone in men and women (not to be confused with its masculinising metabolite in males, *dihydrotestosterone*), rather than adrenalin, appears to be the key chemical for that "special feeling". The same process applies to the trophy hunter, with one notable difference from any other sport – the absence of play. The trophy, the victory, is practically guaranteed, there is little contest and, what is more, the "opponent" is going to die. It is difficult to argue against the proposition that trophy hunting is more about reinforcing dominance than creating joy, more about approval than creativity, more about aggression than assertion. To me, there is no poetry in trophy hunting. The "special feeling", because of the absence of play, is one of power, which means that these hunters can never be satisfied – they can never get enough of it. It becomes a habit, and an addictive one at that.

Assertion, on the other hand, is that rare and precious state of knowing that one's ultimate sense of approval is not externally dependent and that one no longer has to prove oneself. It is as if, as we mature, we become more aware of the difference between fair and unfair play, between hot and cold aggression. We grow up. Perhaps this is the reason why hunters, even the unauthentic ones, put down their guns.

As for the future, there is something that authentic hunters need to do. They need to be a lot more outspoken against the profoundly disturbing practice of "high-fence" or "canned hunting" – the establishment of fenced-in game farms for the purchase, breeding and shooting of wild animals (mostly large herbivores and predators) for the sole purpose of having them shot as trophies. Often baited and in some instances, drugged, these animals have been known to be shot from the back of open vehicles and from behind fences. Who can forget the horrific television footage on canned hunting in 1997 when a lioness on a South African game ranch was shot and killed in front of her cubs?

While many hunters will argue that it is the unscrupulous few, including professional hunters, who have spoiled it for the others, the protest surrounding the entire concept of trophy hunting is growing. Directed not only towards the hunters, but towards the industry that encourages and supports it, the protest is at the same time a plea for an ecological ethic. Ethical hunters stress the importance of a fair chase of the quarry, defining "fairness" as the pursuit, on foot, of a free ranging or enclosed animal that is free to escape its pursuer. The important question, of course, refers to the definition of a canned/trophy hunting operation: how big an area must the land be to ensure a fair chase? To me, the definition of a canned hunting operation is simple: If there is a fence, if there are artificial waterholes and the kill is guaranteed, then the word ethical does not fit. You are dealing with a "canned" hunting operation.

The operators may argue that the selected trophy animals are "usually" past their breeding prime and that they would have been taken by other predators anyway. Why not earn money from them? I will argue that we know little about the kinship and social roles of wild animals once they are beyond their reproductive age. Buffalo are a good example of what we are beginning to discover about the disciplinary, protective and mentoring roles of herd animals. It was always thought that the huge, cantankerous, old bulls (the "dagga boys") were hanging around waiting to die. Not so. It would appear that they continue to play a protective, albeit more distant, educational role in the survival of their kind.

Another argument put forward by breeding operations is that the trophy animals provide a potential gene-pool for rare, exotic or endangered species or that the money earned from trophy hunting pays for the operation as well as providing benefit for local communities such as employment and money for schools and clinics. This may sound plausible, if not noble, but does the end justify the means? And, how much goes toward these noble ends?.

It is well known that one's genes and one's fate are not the same thing. In other words, genetic replication from one generation to another is not a given. It depends on the environment into which the genotype is born. For any creature, its natural environment is a part of its "creatureliness", its cunning, its vigilance, its territoriality, its sexual preferences ... its wildness. Take lions, for example. Is a second or third generation zoo, circus or captive lion the same as its bloodline cousin in the wild? They might look the same, but at the molecular/genetic level, especially with the inevitable interbreeding of close relatives, things may be very different. Two questions need to be asked: what is being bred *into* the gene-pool and with the progressive domestication of the animal, what is being bred *out* of it? Let the history of the breeding and interbreeding of dogs speak for itself. Is this part of the future of wild animals?

Addressing the impact on the gene-pool of domesticating wild animals, the writer and wildlife photographer Ian Michler asks some pointed questions. In the breeding of lions for trophy hunting (although it applies to all animals), he asks: "Are these operators in the process of creating a *domesticated* version of the wild lion? Do we understand the biological, behavioural and philosophical implications of what is going on behind the fences and cages on these farms?" He reminds us that there are at least three broad categories of interaction between humans and wild animals – habituation (when wild animals become familiar with our routine); taming (when we control their feeding behaviour) and domestication (when we control their breeding behaviour). It is a fact that canned-hunting operators are cross breeding lions and tigers to produce "ligers" as trophies. In South Africa they are breeding the rare and recessive lion genotype, the "white lion", for trophy hunters. Antelopes like the Bontebok, *Damaliscus dorcas*, are being crossbred to produce longer horns while others, like the Springbok, *Antidorcas marsupialis*, and the Impala, *Aepcyros melampus*, are being bred for their novel but recessive skin colour genes – all of this for the trophy hunter. Where is the ethic in this? As Michler says, if there is to be any legislation against "canned" hunting it has to be aimed as much at the dealer as at the consumer.

There are two reasons why it is going to be difficult to eradicate trophy hunting. Firstly, the mindset of the trophy hunter will have to change. Secondly, while hunting is not nearly as lucrative as the photographic safari industry, it is nevertheless a profitable one. Money invariably triggers the dark side of human nature and in spite of claims to the contrary, it is a sad fact that – at a price – you can hunt almost any kind of animal you like in the world today, from Bengal tigers and cheetahs to pythons. And yet there are many in the industry who vigorously support trophy hunting and they do so, as I have said, in the name of sustainable utilisation. They say, "animals must pay their way". My question: have they not paid enough, already?

Sustainable utilisation is multi-faceted. From photographic safaris to "green hunting" (paying to participate in scientific research including the darting and relocating of animals) to voluntary work, specified taxation and donations, there are ways of contributing to the financing of conservation other than trophy hunting. To me, this is the way to go. It is part of a bigger picture – one that recognises that we are the keepers of the zoo; that the protection and welfare of the wild is an individual as well as an international responsibility. It begins to take shape when we renew our attitude to wilderness and to wild animals. Trophy hunting is not part of that renewal. Yes, there are indeed more pressing human priorities compared with the protection of wild animals, such as the easing of poverty, but without an appreciation of the importance of wild places in our lives, I believe poverty will take on a different meaning. We will all be the poorer. We will suffer from an impoverishment of soul.

I have no doubt that hunters are generally passionate about the environment. There are also those who are genuinely concerned about issues such as biodiversity, long-term conservation and environmental ethics. I agree with the African president of the Safari Club International – the principal voice of organised hunting – when he calls for dialogue and compromise, and I also believe he is sincere when he says he sees himself to be a co-guardian of the world's natural heritage. However, I do not agree with him when he says that anti-hunting campaigns are attacks on private ownership and personal freedom. The argument is not about human rights but about the nurturing of an ecological intelligence. It is about trying to show the non-sense of killing for that "special feeling" or using an elephant's foot as a waste paper basket, a stool or an umbrella stand. It is about dealing with the welling up and spilling over of rage when we hear that a corporate executive who claims to be an ethical hunter has shot and killed a rare Bongo, *Tragalephus eyryceros*, for his trophy collection. It is what this book is about. The animals are in our blood and in our psyches and they do not exist simply for how useful they can be for human purposes. We can no longer plead ignorance to the genetic evidence found in the unravelling of the human genome. We are dependent on them for more than their meat, their hides or the claim that they exist in order to satisfy the human predatory urge. In psyche and in substance, we are the keepers of the zoo.

We are now face to face with an ethical imperative. Something in us has to say No! Rooted in what the philosophers Hume, Smith and Schopenhauer believed to be an inborn and indestructible instinct for what is fair and what is unfair, to say no is to protest against anything that is damaging or demeaning to a sense of kinship with another – to what we call soul. We can no longer turn our heads, pretending we did not know. I believe there is a code of conduct implicit in our new insights ... one that respects the intrinsic dignity and space of all animals. Let D H Lawrence, in these lines from the poem "Mountain Lion", amplify what I mean:

> Men!
> Two men!
> Men! The only animal in the world to fear!
> ...
> What are they doing here on this vanishing trail?
>
> What is he carrying?
> Something yellow.
> A deer?
> ...
> He smiles, foolishly, as if he were caught doing wrong.

And we smile, foolishly, as if we didn't know.
...
It is a mountain lion,
A long, slim cat, yellow like a lioness.
Dead.

He trapped her this morning, he says, smiling foolishly.
...
And I think in this empty world there was room for me
and a mountain lion.

TO KILL OR NOT TO KILL

And so, is there any justification for hunting, or, put more bluntly, for the killing of animals? To me there is. Meat, from the white of fish and fowl to that of mammalian red, has been a significant part of human survival. To stop the killing or use of animals for food is presently not an option. We need them for more than their spiritual value. However, their nutritional and spiritual value go together. This is the reason why we bless our food. I go along with the hunter who kills for the pot. I would be a hypocrite if I didn't because I eat meat and I eat venison. I can even understand, but I do not condone, the poaching of an animal from a conservancy in order to feed a starving family. I agree with the killing of an animal in self defence, or if it is sick or injured and if to do so is to put it out of its misery. Out of respect for the animals and for biodiversity, I instinctively align myself to a philosophy of non-interference rather than culling and yet, I cannot argue with absolute conviction against the need to manage sustainable populations of animals confined to fenced-in grazing and browsing areas. I have learned enough about culling to know that it is a contentious issue and that it should always remain so. "We cannot wait for the research" should never be an excuse to go ahead with the perceived need to cull. We must learn to wait. Culling should never be based on the notion of "ideal" numbers of animals. Instead, it should be based on an understanding of the natural history of the animal, its breeding cycles, its peaks and vales, the terrain of the animal, climatic rhythms, natural diseases, species interactions and biodiversity.

It is important to remember that animals are in a continuous process of adaptation. In many instances they will adjust to changing climatic and geographical conditions without our intervention. Time constraints, deadlines and ultimatums are human constructs and they seldom work in the wild. It is not always easy to see the potential order in what is often interpreted as chaos and destruction, for example, the impact of the growing populations of elephants on the trees in Africa's game reserves. Respect the process. Look at fallen trees differently. See in their twisted shapes the potential ecosystems of termites, ants and other insects, butterflies, reptiles, birds and the developing food-chains in and around the decaying trees. See the space created by the fallen tree as space for the grasses that feed the herbivores. An area of fallen trees may not look aesthetically pleasing, but when seen in an ecological context, the dead trees come "alive". Yes, elephants will die, as will other animals – they might starve and their reproductive cycles will alter, but this is not new in the wild. We should know by now that when we interfere, we often make the situation worse. The introduction of artificial watering holes, as well as the erection of protective fences is bound to have an effect on the migratory and population dynamics of elephants and other animals. Then again, there may be times when we need to cull, in which case, let it be done in the knowledge that the slain animal is not a trophy.

Finally, the code of conduct I am referring to applies equally to non-hunting activities, especially to the cameramen and crews responsible for the increasing number of dubious wildlife documentaries making their appearance on our television screens. While their trophies remain alive, wrestling crocodiles and pythons and doing handstands in front of elephants sends a clear message – the activity is about human dominance over animals. This may not be the conscious intention of the human players in these documentaries, but it is how it comes across and

I believe deep down they know it. Thank heavens for those, like The Save The Rhino Foundation, who will not submit to the demands of these cameramen. On one particular film-shoot in Namibia, the on-site members of the foundation refused to provoke a desert-adapted black rhinoceros, *Diceros bicornis bicornis*, into charging the photographer. Of course, it would have made a great shot. After all, it is the shot that sells the footage. In instances like this, the crew would argue that they mean no harm and that the footage is educational. However, whenever wildlife situations are manipulated to suit the photographer, the harm is already done – animals' fear and suspicion of humans is reinforced and at the same time the viewers, many of whom are well informed about animal behaviour, find the obvious commercialism repellant.

As for its educational significance, the manipulated human-animal interaction is seldom the way things really are in the wild. One of the problems with this misperception is that uninformed visitors to wildlife areas, many of them paying high prices to be there, expect the same kind of interaction and feel cheated when they don't get it. These same visitors often incite guides and game rangers, many of whom are young and eager to please, to break the rules by getting too close to, or even provoking animals into charging. It has happened to me. Most don't succumb to the pressure. However, there is another group of guides and rangers who need no incitement. Perhaps out of boredom, familiarity, or sheer machismo they wittingly break the professional code of conduct and with it their pact with the wild.

And so, when last did you have a sense of the "No" feeling – the feeling that what we are doing at the human-animal interface is inappropriate, that it is unfair or that it is simply unethical? Does that feeling have a voice when it comes to trophy hunting, to manipulated wildlife photography and documentaries, to the sale of ivory, the logging of the rain forests and the unbridled harvesting of the seas? And will your voice be heard?

Will the mindset change? Will it come from within, or, when the evidence against the hunting of any animal for trophy purposes is properly understood, will it need to be legislated against? Remember that colossal gesture on 18 July 1989 when the then president of Kenya set to flames US$ 3 million worth (at that time) of ivory. None of us can escape that message ... some things are simply not for sale.

I am a pilgrim of the future on the way back
from a journey made entirely in the past.

Teilhard de Chardin

Breathe one last time
your wild breath into me
that I may not forget you,
that I may remember who I am ...

Barbara Fairhead

10
HEADING OUT – COMING HOME

THE TWENTIETH CENTURY WILL BE REMEMBERED FOR MANY REASONS – the radio, the telephone, the automobile, aircraft, space travel, the harnessing and unleashing of nuclear power, cinematography, television, computers, the internet. It will be remembered for its weapons, its wars, for antibiotics, psychoanalysis, organ transplants and the unravelling of the human genome. Sadly, it will also be remembered as the century in which the ways of the wild, the natural migrations, their habitat and the capacity of the animals to find their own balance with the land, changed forever. The reason for this is inescapable – the human factor – our insecurity, our arrogance, our ignorance. With few exceptions we have become the victims of our intellectual success, and it shows. By continuing to distance ourselves from Nature and from our fellow soul-makers, we, too, have lost our sense of balance. We suffer from a loss of soul.

It is true, we've come a long way since that mythological day when Apollo announced that first great ecological admonition – know thyself. And yet we hardly know ourselves at all. This is ironic, given that our search for who and what we are has been almost obsessive. We have technology that can take us into what we believe to be the very heart of matter – machines that can measure one billionth of one billionth of a metre (10^{-19}). As if this is not enough, we are presently assembling in Geneva, Switzerland, a twenty-seven kilometre-long accelerator, or particle-smasher, that will add an extra power of ten to our microscopic search for meaning. Known as the Large Hadron Collidor, the temperatures created in the particle collisions will be around one billion times that of the centre of the sun. Why are we doing this? By attempting to emulate the conditions that are believed to have existed less than one billionth of a second after the Big Bang, we hope to find among the scattered particles, the *graviton* or Higgs boson – the so-called God particle. According to the Standard Model of particle physics, the graviton, in the same way that DNA is the carrier of genes, is the generator and carrier of mass and gravity. The finding of this particle, we believe, will go a long way toward a better understanding of "dark matter" including the antigravity properties of "dark energy".

With technology that can detect galaxies as far away as ten thousand million light years from us, we are searching in the other direction too. In the 1970s, in a poignant statement of how alone we are in the known universe, two separate Pioneer spacecraft took off into deep space carrying with them an engraved likeness of *Homo sapiens sapiens*, together with a fugue by Johan Sebastian Bach and a message of "hello" from Earth. As I write, those spaceships are already far beyond our solar system. Their journey, so far, has been profoundly silent.

As exciting and as metaphysically balanced as these two directions have been, they are essentially journeys that detract, in this crucial time of human history, from perhaps the most exciting and the most essential journey of them all – the inner one. Like the inward-hooking thorn of the ziziphus, this is the complementary journey, the one that will bring us face to face with the world and with ourselves. The images of macro and micro space are within us. It is time to give them a life that is immediate and specific. To do this, we need to develop an intelligence that is ecological.

I have attempted to describe ecological intelligence as a way of understanding and articulating our evolutionary links with all living things, the debt that we owe to the Earth and the contribution of wild things to the evolution of human consciousness. It is an intelligence that can grasp the significance of the three-fold instruction of Apollo. To me, these admonitions should be on the wall of every corporate and conservation boardroom. They should be part of the vision statements of developers and entrepreneurs, a mental map for lawyers, engineers, doctors and teachers, as well as the silent mantra for every environmentalist. As we continue to live the questions surrounding our concerns for the Earth, I believe this intelligence will continue to define itself.

We are the human animal and there are profound ecological responsibilities that come with this privilege. We are the only creatures who can say yes and no to traditions, religions and conventional wisdom. But what is the point of this if we can't say yes and no to the timing and the intensity of our own threat displays, our compulsions, conformity and our territorial acquisitiveness? We are not the masters of our fate and we are not going to be rescued from the ecological predicament of our time, either. We can, however, without detaching ourselves from it, rise above it. We can change ourselves by changing our behaviour, says the philosopher and naturalist Richard Rorty – especially our linguistic behaviour. Freedom of speech is not simply a freedom to think and to say what you wish, but to speak for yourself, to speak from the heart and to be accountable for your words.

I have introduced poetry as the language that can best convey the essence of an ecological intelligence, for it is the only language I know that can adequately redress the Human-Nature split. Disobedient to the force of gravity, as the poet Simone Weil puts it, it is not only a language but an attitude. It is a language and an attitude that takes us to the edge of our imagination, bridging the gap between science and non-science, between the actual and the imagined. It speaks from the heart. I hope there was at least one poem quoted in this book that spoke to you in the way that all of them have spoken to me.

Poets may or may not be the "the unacknowledged legislators of the world", as Shelley claimed them to be, but their work continues to have a profound influence on our thoughts. "And it is because of the cataclysms and transformations of the past century," wrote the literary critic Lord Gorell, that poetry, "the undying, is more, and not less, necessary." Poetry above all, because it looks beyond the surface of things, is a language that takes us deep into the world and because of this, in the words of the literary scholar Mark Freeman, "the world is always capable of being thought anew". And then there is Wordsworth's admonition: "On all poets is laid the duty of hope." If this is so, as I believe it is, then poetry is the language that, for now at least, can best define an intelligence that is ecological.

We have looked at the wake-up calls of the past millennium, identifying their areas of impact – physics, cosmology, evolution and depth psychology. Copernicus redefined the centre of our solar system and with it the relegation of the Earth to one of a handful of planets. Galileo discovered that we are not the only planet with a moon and then came Newton's laws of an absolute Universe. "I am standing on the shoulders of giants," said Newton in acknowledgement of those who had helped him to formulate his laws. Newton's laws went unchallenged for two hundred years until Einstein came along with his dual theories of relativity. "I am standing on the shoulders of Newton," said Einstein. Suddenly, there were no absolutes of space, mass or time. Light travelled in waves *or* particles – it all depended, at the subatomic level, on the intention of the observer. What kind of a psychological truth was this? And now we know that the speed of light is no longer a universal limit.

Einstein's genius opened the way for Quantum Theory and with it the stunning realization that the influence of atomic particles, one upon the other, irrespective of distance, is instantaneous. What is more, they do not move from one point to another – they manifest at their new locality as if they had always been there. This gave credence to the probability of quantum fields, to field thinking, and to the socio-biological notion of a web of life.

Darwin's theory of the evolution of species gave us something to ponder. I believe it was something to celebrate. The decoding of the human genome tells us that we are indeed related to the animals, the insects and the plants and that, like it or not, Earth is where we belong. Once again, the old poets were right. Edward Abbey, in his book, *Desert Solitaire*, puts it this way:

> All men are brothers, we like to say. Half wishing some-
> times in secret it were not true. And is the evolutionary

line from protozoan to Spinoza any less certain? That also may be true. We are obliged therefore to spread the news, painful and bitter though it may be for some to hear ... that all living things are kindred.

Yes ... there's a menagerie inside our ribs, beneath our bony skulls, says Carl Sandburg, and we are the keepers of the zoo. Is this not a good enough reason to be alive? Could we ask for a privilege more meaningful than this?

And then came those great pioneers of psychology, Freud and Jung. Between them they gave us the first meaningful maps for the journey into the human psyche. They both understood the importance of the unconscious part of our psyche in our daily lives, as well as its nocturnal language – our dreams. It was Jung, however, who understood its evolutionary significance. Seeing it as more than a personal unconscious, he called it the collective unconscious. Within it, he said, are the archetypes – the guiding, psychological motifs and images that have steered us through our two-and-a-half-million-year tenure as a social species. Not only did he understand the evolutionary roots of human nature, he understood what comes with it – our dark side. He called this psychological blind spot our shadow.

It is hard to accept that the intellect, which has made the human animal appear so clever, so ingenious, invariably fails to recognise what comes with it – the early steps of its undoing. It is difficult to acknowledge that a blind spot comes along with the "all-seeing" human retina. And yet if we know this, then it is not difficult to see within the blind spot of kinship recognition and the evolutionary fear of strangers, the early dynamics of in-groups and out-groups, of racism and xenophobia. Addressing our shadow has been an important part of this book.

To rediscover ourselves in Nature, a sense of our evolutionary history is going to be important but it is not sufficient. It is sobering enough to remember from where and how far we have come, but it is even more sobering to consider where we might be headed. Viewed from a perspective of cosmic time, our history of adaptation and advancement as a species has been a relatively short one. But has it been successful? In terms of technological advancement, it would appear so, but is this really the case? Adapt we have, but does it not make sense that successful adaptation should be a win-win situation, or are we still stuck in the Old Testament notion of having to have dominion over every living thing? We have yet to get our language right. Successful adaptation does not mean dominance and neither does it mean forever.

Natural selection is often misunderstood as being a polite analogy for the outdated but deeply ingrained notion of the "survival of the fittest", and with it, the idea that the different species on Earth exist in hierarchies of dominance. It is not about that at all. Instead, it is a process of give and take, governed by the co-existence of species. It accounts for the way organisms successfully fit into and with the environment. The very essence of natural selection is that organisms come to match their habitats by being "the fittest available" or "the fittest yet": they are not the "best imaginable". Technological progress, therefore, is a misleading gauge of successful adaptation. In spite of its apparent benefits we have failed to acknowledge the shadow that comes with technology and as a result are in danger of becoming less fit in terms of the definition above. We need to answer Antonio Machado's question: "What have you done with the garden that was entrusted to you?" Honour the gods said Apollo. Be aware of the intelligence in every living thing. And after you have done that, ask permission to enter the space of the "other".

In evolutionary terms, it is too early to speak about the successful adaptation of the human animal to this little planet. Compared with the long, imperial reign of the dinosaurs, let alone that of our scaly cousins the crocodiles, the snakes and the birds, we are pipsqueaks in the evolutionary "hall of fame". And yet few would argue the astonishing impact on Earth of the creature that suddenly stood up, freeing not only his hands to grasp the Earth's elements, but a mind that could mould the elements, shape them and make symbols of them.

We are an Earth-bound species. We are born out of it and we return to it. What we do to it, we do to ourselves. It is in this light that I have difficulty in believing that an ecological intelligence is something that is being reclaimed – an implication that our failed ecological strategies reflect some kind of historical fall from grace. I doubt that there has ever been a "golden age" of ecology in the world, a time when men and women lived in perfect harmony with the Earth. Instead, out of a dire necessity, I believe it to be an intelligence that is evolving. The word perfection is foreign to evolution and so is the word harmony, which implies a world devoid of dissonance and tension. In other words, paradise has probably never existed outside of the human imagination. Of course we miss the "good old days" when the rains came, when firewood was on one's doorstep and people were generally happier than they are today. I don't think I am being cynical when I say that human memories tend to be selective, but we forget that our modern environmental and political predicaments are rooted in those so-called "good old days". In other words, our forefathers are also in the dock. Like Oedipus, they should have known. What will our children say of us? Are we able to look beyond our own lifetime?

The future of humans as an interdependent species is precarious. It is difficult to name any other force quite as threatening to the planet as the growing human population and, with it, the increasing pressure on the land for housing and food production. The population factor is a challenge that is perplexing, painful and awesome. Douglas Chadwick, writing in 1992, put the population bomb into perspective:

> It took more than a million years for human numbers to add up to 1 billion. That mark was reached around the year AD 1800, two centuries ago. The second billion was added during just the next 130 years. Barely thirty years later, the third billion had arrived. Fifteen years later, the total was 4 billion. We reached our current 5 billion in another dozen years.

By the year 2000, we had six billion people on Earth. With this trend we can expect ten billion by the middle of the century. We have taken the Genesis admonition to be fruitful and multiply too literally.

To be fruitful is not only to be biologically fertile, but to be fruitful and fertile in our thoughts also. To multiply is not restricted to arithmetic, either. It does not only mean producing more of the same thing. Rather, it is to be expansive in our thinking, to be flexible and multifaceted. It is to develop the capacity to embrace the multiplicity of all living things and living expressions on Earth. If anything, we are the ones who need to be a little more subdued, and by this I mean not only the subduing of our growing numbers, but of downplaying our inflated notions of human divinity.

And so, what are we to do about it? Can history help us? I'm afraid not. The present population of human beings on Earth is unprecedented. Let us not forget that. What we can do, however, is to become more aware of the harsh social realities of human reproduction. We would do well to remember that people who are poor tend to have more children than those who are materially better off. Paradoxically, it is part of their survival. Insurance and retirement annuities are the security of the "haves" and the inhabitants of the welfare state; children are the security of the "have-nots" in the developing nations. Carl Sagan, in his erudite and humbling book, *Billions and Billions*, wrote:

> There is a well-documented, world-wide correlation between poverty and high birth rates. In little countries and big countries, in communist countries, Catholic countries and Muslim countries, Western countries and Eastern countries – in almost all these cases, exponential population growth slows down or stops when grinding poverty disappears. This is called the demographic transition. It is in the urgent long-term interest of the human species that every place on Earth achieves this demographic transition. This is why helping other countries to become self-

sufficient is not only elementary human decency, but is also in the self-interest of those richer nations able to help.

Saving the lives of children and prolonging our own life spans does not make objective sense, and yet no one would dare advocate that we abandon our attempts to do so. There is something in our psyche that will not allow it. We are survivors and we are a social species. We do care, but we are going to have to learn to care differently – about the land, about the animals and about ourselves.

The choice is ours and it has to be made now. As E O Wilson says, we have to decide whether to accept our corrosive and risky behaviour as the unavoidable price of population and economic growth, or to take stock of ourselves and search for a new environmental ethic. Urging us to look deep within ourselves and to decide what we wish to become, he chooses the hard path – volitional evolution. "Alter the biological nature of the human species in any direction you wish, or you may leave it alone," he says, "either way, genetic evolution is about to become conscious and volitional, and usher in a new epoch in the history of life." It is going to present the most profound intellectual and ethical choices humanity has ever faced, which means, above all, that we are going to have to learn how to say yes and no to the forces of human nature. Without being naïve, we must adopt a stance that promises a concern for the intelligence and well-being of every living thing.

The zoologist Jonathan Kingdon puts it this way: "we must remake ourselves in some fashion that retains and develops the countless benefits of technology and culture, yet does not cut us off from or destroy all the physical processes that created us as animals." And then there is that other imaginative and courageous spokesman for the Earth, James Lovelock. Out of a deep concern for the human impact on our planet, he issues a bold challenge. If, because of the evolution of the cortex, human beings can reflect upon themselves, then we need to see ourselves as the reflecting cortex of the Earth. "Through human beings," he says poetically, "the Earth can become conscious of itself.

In this book I have made several references to the traditional hunter-gatherers of the world, more especially to Africa's ancient nomads, the Kalahari "bushmen". As we review our present ecological thinking, we might be mistaken into believing that their way of life is a model for the ecological intelligence that we are trying to define. The "bushmen" no longer live in the traditional hunter-gatherer way that they used to, but even if they could, it is obvious that theirs might have been a life to be admired, but not necessarily envied. Compared with our world of running water, electricity, flush-toilets, and including our pursuit of material comforts, instant gratification and insurance against the unknown, their physical existence was a tough one. There is no turning back. Very few of us would be willing, let alone able, to free ourselves from our first-world cosmologies and comforts in favour of their spartan, but by no means uncivilised lifestyles and life-views. To reflect on this is a reminder that the intelligence we seek will be meaningless unless it can be translated beyond the worlds of traditional hunter-gatherers into our complex world of cultivation and consumerism. We have to re-examine what Jacquetta Hawkes once called "the fetish of the standard of living", replacing it with "a standard of values, in which beauty, comeliness, and the possibility of solitude have a high place among human needs."

We must learn to be poor in the right way in order to become richer in the right way, says the Indian social ecologist, R Guha. In other words, to favour wiser ways of living off the land and the sea, we have to be more careful in differentiating between what we want and what we need. The "pantry complex" – taking more than we need – is deeply ingrained in our evolution. It is part of our opportunistic or, to be less polite, our scavenging nature. Separating needs from wants is poetic thinking but it will mean nothing unless we can make it workable.

Barry Lopez, in his hard-hitting book, *The Rediscovery of North America*, does not mince his words when he deals with the subject of human greed. He calls it a crisis both of culture and character. "We have an obligation," he says, well aware of the revolutionary significance of his words, "to develop a hard and focused anger at what continues to be done to the land, not so people can survive, but so that a relatively few can amass wealth." We are obliged therefore to nurture an intelligence capable of making the shift from short-term survival thinking – me versus you – to one that consciously grasps the long-term significance of I and Thou. In essence, it requires that we be careful of our language, and refuse to be seduced by jargon and slogans such as "ethical hunting", "sustainable utilisation", "downsizing", "eco-friendly", "transparency", "biodegradable", "development" and "growth".

While it carries such positive connotations when used in an intellectual or economic context, the word "growth" is also the name for a tumour. Cancer is a condition where host cells become autonomous and multiply. It spreads, it invades, it occupies, eventually killing the host. We fight it, we look for and claim all kinds of causes for it along a bio-psycho-sociological spectrum and yet, unless it is caught early, there is often very little that we can do about its relentless course. Notwithstanding the genetic influence regarding the natural history of various illnesses, could it be that cancer is one of the diseases of our time, our niche and our evolution? And if so, is there anything we can learn from it, for it is indeed a chilling metaphor for human behaviour?

As with any life threatening illness, perhaps it is this: as we face our death, it inevitably changes our lives. It opens us to many possible outcomes. It challenges us to live our dying and to say goodbye to those we have loved. It reminds us that death is not an enemy but an inevitable turning point in life, a shift in a molecular-chemical dance as old as the universe itself. Jung, more than half a century ago, had already come to the conclusion that the meaning of life lay in a complete adjustment to the laws of nature ... with a gradual maturing toward death as a final goal. "Death must be regarded as the fulfilment of life's meaning and its real aim," he said in 1934. In a way that one might regard the "life" of a subatomic particle, he believed that the human psyche was deeply involved in a "time ... and spaceless form of existence which might symbolically and inadequately be called eternal." To me, the notion of dust to dust is poetry and science. It is at the heart of what it means to think molecular.

Some years ago, while working as a doctor in a small mining town along the west coast of South Africa, I was witness on the same night to what could be regarded as life's two great mysteries – birth and death. One of my patients, a man in the terminal phases of a bronchial carcinoma, was breathing heavily as he slipped in and out of a coma. Seated at his bedside was his wife. She was holding his hand, fully aware of the warmth that was slipping away from her. Standing opposite her, I held his other hand, my fingers acutely aware of the pulse that was now racing toward its ultimate fate.

"She's ready, doctor," said the nurse who had opened the door just enough to show her face. It was a half-whisper, with enough urgency in it to show that she was serious. Down the corridor a young mother in the final stages of labour was close to delivery. Excusing myself I headed for the labour ward, rolling up my sleeves as I made my way through the doors of the delivery room towards the wash-hand basins.

Fifteen minutes later, a healthy, ten-fingered child was warmly wrapped and cradled in the arms of her exhausted mother. I headed back to the dying man and to his wife who greeted me with a silent, imploring look. He was still with us. About half-an-hour later he let out a long sigh. It was his final breath and it coincided with a sound I will never forget. It was the cry of a newly born infant echoing down the corridor. Later that night, I wrote this poem, "Deliverance".

Tonight is my night she said
I can feel it deep inside
And tonight is my night he said
I can feel there is nowhere to hide
The pain comes and goes she said
This life deep inside moves about
The pain comes and goes he said
This life deep inside wants out
My breathing is deep she said
With labour there's so much pain
And my breathing is pain he said

I will not labour again
I am ripe to deliver she said
I can feel it all below
And I am ripe to deliver he said
There's a need deep inside to let go
O what a song she said
It is life and the young child cried
O what a song he said
It is life and the old body died

Is there any cheer in this speculative analysis of our fate and of what it means to be the human animal? I think there is. It is in that tiny fraction of the genome that makes our consciousness different from that of a chimpanzee. The human animal can make choices that no other creature, as far as I am aware, can make. We can choose to drift into oblivion, to turn our heads, pretending we did not see, or we can refuse to be victims, as Oedipus did. We can choose the hard path – the one that demands accountability: the one that demands that we give beauty and meaning, in our own way, to the Earth and to the countless living things that share it with us.

Finally, we can choose to turn our usual image of the human animal at the apex of creation upside down. Instead of seeing ourselves at the point, let's imagine ourselves instead at the open edge of a rose, a spiral shell or a cup into which we can look to see all things taking shape and where the stem and the edge are one. Let's try to imagine ourselves as the living equivalents of an ark upon a great evolutionary sea. Let's become conscious of the animals that we have on board with us and of what they mean to us – that we need them as much and probably more than they need us. If we are divine, then so is every other creature on this planet. We have no right to drive any of them into extinction. Instead, let's learn to say thank you to these older brothers and sisters.

Does the image of the ziziphus speak to you? Do the poets and those ancient admonitions of Apollo – to know thyself, to do no thing in

excess and to honour the gods, make sense? Is an ecological intelligence possible? If so, then say YES, quickly. This could be the last
watch, and there are things to do.

BIBLIOGRAPHY

Abbey, Edward, 1968: Desert Solitaire.
Random House, New York
Abram, David, 1996: The Spell of the
Sensuous. Random House, Toronto
Anderson, John M, 2001: Towards Gondwana
Alive: Pretoria
Ardrey, Robert, 1967: The Territorial
Imperative: Fontana Books, Glasgow
Atkinson, Rita, L; Atkinson, Richard C;
Smith, Edward E; Hilgard, Ernest R,
1987: Introduction to Psychology. Harcourt,
Florida
Bateson, Gregory, 1979: Mind and Nature –
A necessary Unity. Fontana, London
Begon, Harper, Townsend: Ecology
Bickerton, D, 1995: Language and Human
Behavior. University of Washington Press
Blixen, Karen, 1937: Out of Africa. Penguin
Books, Middlesex, England
Bly, Robert, 1995: News of the Universe.
Library of Congress Cataloging, USA
1981: The Selected Poetry of Rainer Maria
Rilke. HarperCollins, New York
Bly, Robert; Hillman, James; Meade,
Michael, 1992: The Rag and Bone Shop of
the Heart – Poems for Men. HarperCollins,
New York
Briggs, John & Peat, David, 1989. Harper &
Row, New York
Bronowski, I, 1973: The Ascent of Man.
BBC London
Bullock, Alan, Stallybrass, Oliver & Tumbley,
Stephen, 1988: The Fontana Dictionary of
Modern Thought. Fontana Books, London
Campbell, Joseph, 1984: The Way of the
Animal Powers. Times Books, London
Camus, Albert: The Myth of Sisyphus, Ethics,
1994 by Peter Singer, Oxford University Press
Capra, Fritjof,
1975: The Tao of Physics. Shambhala, London
1988: Uncommon Wisdom and 1982: The
Turning Point. Simon & Schuster, New York
Charbonneau-Lassay, Louis, 1940: The
Bestiary of Christ. Desclee, De Bruwer & Cel.
Coetzee, J M, 1999: The Lives of Animals.
Princeton University Press, New Jersey, USA
Conrad, Joseph, 1902: Heart of Darkness.
Penguin Books, London
Croall, Stephen; Rankin, William, 1982:

Ecology for Beginners. Writers & Readers
Publishing, London
Crow, T J, 1997: Schizophrenia as Failure of
Hemispheric Dominance for Language.
Elsevier Science Ltd., TINS, Vol. 20, No. 8,
pp 339–343
Damasio, Antonio, 2003: Looking for Spinoza.
Harcourt, Orlando, Floridea USA
Davies, Paul, 2002: That Mysterious Flow.
Scientific American, September 2002,
Vol. 287, No. 3
Dawkins, Richard, 1986: The Blind
Watchmaker: Penguin Books, London
De Chardin, Teilhard, 1959: The
Phenomenon of Man. Harper & Torch
Books, New York
De Waal, Frans, 1996: Good Natured – The
Origins of Right and Wrong in Humans and
other Animals. Harvard University Press,
Cambridge, Massachusetts
Dossey, Larry, 1982: Space, Time and
Medicine. Shambhala Pub., Boulder, Colorado.
Eliade, Mercia, 1964: Shamanism – Archaic
Techniques of Ecstasy. Penguin Books
Limited, London
Elkington, John, 1997: Cannibals with Forks.
Capstone Publishing Ltd, Oxford
Estes, Richard Despard, 1997: The Behaviour
Guide to African Mammals. Russel Friedman
Books, Halfway House, South Africa
Fairhead, Barbara, 2001: Word and Bead –
The Presentation of a Journey: Private
Collection, Cape Town
Foster, Craig, Foster, Damon, 2001: The Great
Dance – A Hunter's Story: Aardvaark/
Earthrise/Liquid Pictures, South Africa
Fuller, Buckminster R, 1981: Critical Path.
Hutchinson Publishing, London
Funston, Malcolm, 1993: Bushveld Trees.
Fernwood Press, Cape Town
Ginn, P J; McIlron, WG, Milstein, P le S,
1991: The Complete Book of Southern
African Birds. Struik Publishing,
Cape Town
Gould, Stephen Jay; The Flamingo's Smile,
1985. W W Norton and Co., New York
Graham, John, 2002: Straw Dogs – Thoughts
on Humans and other Animals. Granta
Books, London

Hauser, Marc, 2000: Wild Minds – What
Animals Really Think. Penguin, London
Hawkes, Jacquetta, 1953: A Land. The Cresset
Press, London
Hawking, Stephen, 1988: A Brief History of
Time. Bantam Press, London
Heaney, Seamus,
1999: Beowulf. Faber & Faber, London
1995: The Redress of Poetry. HarperCollins,
Canada
Hillman, James, 1975: Loose Ends and 1979:
The Puer Papers. Spring Publications,
Dallas (now Putnam)
1997: The Dream Animal. Chronicle Books,
San Francisco
Horrobin, David, 2001: The Madness of Adam
& Eve. Transworld Pub, London
Johnson, Paul, 1983: A History of the Modern
World. Weidenfeld & Nicolson Ltd, London
Jung, Carl G,
1964: Man and his Symbols. Alders Books, UK
1962: Memories, Dreams, Reflections.
William Collins & Sons, Glasgow
1928: The Relations between the Ego and
the Unconscious, from Two Essays on
Analytical Psychology, CW7
1951: The Shadow from Aion – CW9
1957: The Undiscovered Self – from
Civilization in Transition – CW10
1959: Good and Evil in Analytical Psychology
– from Civilization in Transition – CW10
1938/1940: Psychology and Religion – from
Psychology and Religion: West and East – CW11
1952: Synchronicity: An acausal connecting
principle – from The Structure and
Dynamics of the Psyche – CW8
Laing, R D, 1959: The Divided Self. Penguin
Books, Middlesex, England
1967: The Politics of Experience
Lawrence, D H, 1921: Psychoanalysis and the
Unconscious. Penguin
Leakey, Richard; Lewin, Roger,
1992: Origins Reconsidered. Abacus Books, UK
1996: The Sixth Extinction. Orion Books, UK
Leunig, Michael, 1999: Goatperson and other
tales. Penguin Books, Australia
Liebenberg, Louis, 1990: The Art of Tracking
– The Origins of Science. David Philip
Publishers, Cape Town
Lopez, Barry,
1986: Arctic Dreams – Imagination and

Desire in a Northern Landscape. Macmillan
Publishers, New York
1978: Men and Wolves. Simon & Schuster,
New York
1990: Rediscovery of North America.
Vintage Books, New York
Lorenz, Konrad, 1952: King Solomon's Ring.
Methmen Books, London
Lovegrove, Barry, 1993: The Living Deserts
of Southern Africa. Fernwood Press,
Cape Town
Lovelock, James, 1979: Gaia – A New Look
at Life on Earth. Oxford University Press
Maclean, Norman, 1976: A River Runs
Through It. University of Chicago Press
Magee, Bryan, 1973: Popper. Fontana Books,
London
Malan, Robin, 1986: New Inscapes, Oxford
University Press, Southern Africa
Marais, Eugene, 1973: The Soul of the White
Ant. Jonathan Ball, Johannesburg
Margulis, Lynn, 1999: Symbiotic Planet –
A New Look At Evolution. Basic Books, USA
McCallum (theory), cited in Psyche and
Substance, 1982: North Atlantic Books, USA
McCallum, Ian,
2000: Thorns to Kilimanjaro. David Philip
Publishers, Cape Town
1999: Wild Gifts. Creda Press, Cape Town
McNutt, John; Boggs, Lesley; Heldring,
Helene; Hamman, David, 1996: Running Wild
– Dispelling the Myths of the African Wild
Dog. Southern Books, Halfway House, RSA
Meltzer, D, 1986: Studies in Extended
Metapsychology. Clunie Press
Meredith, Martin, 2001: Africa's Elephant –
A Biography. Hodder & Stroughton, London
Moore, Patrick, 1994: Stars of the Southern
Skies. Bateman Books, Auckland
Mills, Gus & Hes, Lex: 1997: The Mammals of
Southern Africa. Struik Publishers, Cape Town
Morris, Desmond,
1967: The Naked Ape. Corgi Books, London
1969: The Human Zoo. Corgi Books, London
Mutwa, Credo, 1996: Isilwane – The Animal.
Struik Publishers, Cape Town
Nash, Roderick F, 1982: Wilderness and the
American Mind. Yale University Press
Neruda, Pablo, 1974: Memoirs. Souvenir Press
Limited, London
Neumann, Erich, 1954: The Origins and

History of Consciousness. Bollingen Foundation, New York

Panskepp, Jaak, 1998: Affective Neuroscience – The Foundations of Human and Animal Emotions. Oxford University Press, New York

Pasachoff, Jay M, 1981: Contemporary Astronomy. Saunders College Publishing, New York

Pirsig, Robert, 1974: Zen and the Art of Motorcycle Maintenance. Vintage Books, UK

Poole, Michael, 1995: Beliefs & Values in Science Education. Open University Press, Buckingham

Rakoff, Vivian, 1992: The Psychiatrist and the Myth of the Healer, Canadian Journal of Medicine, Vol. 37

Rayner, Eric, 1992: Matching, Attunement and the Psychoanalytical Dialogue: International Journal of Psychoanalysis, 73/39

Rilke, Rainer Maria, 1981: The Selected Poetry of Rainer Maria Rilke. HarperCollins, New York

Rohman, Chris, 2000: Dictionary of Important Ideas and Thinkers. Arrow Books, London

Roodt, Veronica, 1998: Trees and Shrubs of the Okavango Delta. Briza Publications, Arcadia

Russell, Peter, 1982: The Awakening Earth – Our Next Evolutionary Leap. Routledge, London

Sagan, Carl, 1997: Billions and Billions. Random House, New York

Sanders, N K, cited in Straw Dogs (see Graham, John: 2002)

Schroeder, Herbert, 1991: The Spiritual Aspect of Nature – A Perspective from Depth Psychology: Proceedings of N E Recreation Research Conference, Saratoga, USA

Shakespeare, William: Hamlet. Wordsworth Editions, London

Shalamov, Vartam, cited in Straw Dogs (see Graham, John: 2002)

Sheldrake, Rupert, 1999: Dogs that know when their owners are coming home. Arrow Books, UK

Singer, Peter, 1994: Ethics. Oxford University Press, Oxford

Smuts, J C, 1926: Holism and Evolution. NGS Press, Cape Town

Sophocles: Oedipus the King. Penguin Classics

Solms, Mark, Turnbull, Oliver, 2002: The Brain and the Inner World. Other Press, New York.

Stapleton, Michael, 1978: Greek and Roman Mythology. Hamlyn Publishing Group, London

Stevens, Anthony; Price, John, 1996: Evolutionary Psychiatry. Routledge, London

Stevens, Anthony, 1998: An Intelligent Person's guide to Psychotherapy. Redwood Books, London

Sykes, Bryan, 2001: The Seven Daughters of Eve. Bantam Press, London

Tattersall, Ian, 2000: Once We Were Not Alone, Scientific American, Vol. 282, No. 1

Trivers, Robert, 1971: The Evolution of Reciprocal Altruism, Quarterly Review of Biology, 46

Van der Post, Laurens, 1955: The Dark Eye in Africa. Hogarth Press Ltd, London

Wagoner, David, 1999: Traveling Light: Collected and New Poems. University of Illinois Press.

Walker, Alan; Shipman, Pat, 1997: The Wisdom of Bones – In Search of Human Origins. Wiedengeld & Nicolson, UK

Watson, Lyall, 2002: Elephantoms. W W Norton & Company, New York
1973: Supernature, 1975: Dark Nature. Hazel & Stoughton, London

Watson, Stephen, 1991: Return of the Moon. Carrefour, Cape Town

Whalen, Paul, 1998: Journal of Neuroscience Vol. 18: 411–418

Whyte, David, 2001: Crossing the Unknown Sea: Work as a Pilgrimage of Identity. Riverhead Books, New York

Whitmont, Edward, C, 1980: Psyche and Substance: Essays on Homeopathy in the Light of Jungian Psychology. North Atlantic Books, Berkeley, California

Wilson, Colin, 1966: Introduction to the New Existentialism. Hutchinson & Co., London

Wilson, E O, 1984: Biophilia – The Human Bond with other Species, Library of Congress Cataloging, USA
1999: Consilience. Random House, New York
2002: The Future of Life. Abacus, London

Winston, Robert, 2002: Human Instinct – How our Primeval Impulses shape our Modern Lives. Random House, London

Zohar, Danah, 1983: Through the Time Barrier – A Study in Precognition and Modern Physics. Paladin Books, London

Zukav, Gary, 1979: The Dancing Wu Li Masters. Rider Hutchinson, London

INDEX

242

Index of first lines of poems